King Henry the 8th

By William Shakespeare

Edited by Julien Coallier

Copyright Julien Coallier 2012

All Rights Reserved.

Scenes

Act I – Page 11

Scene 1 London. An ante-chamber in the palace.

Scene 2 The same. The council-chamber.

Scene 3 An ante-chamber in the palace.

Scene 4 A Hall in York Place.

Act II – Page 43

Scene 1 Westminster. A street.

Scene 2 An ante-chamber in the palace.

Scene 3 An ante-chamber of the Queen's apartments.

Scene 4 A hall in Black-Friars.

Act III – Page 75

Scene 1 London. Queen Katharine's apartments.

Scene 2 Ante-chamber to King Henry VIII's apartment.

Act IV – Page 105

Scene 1 A street in Westminster.

Scene 2 Kimbolton.

Act V – Page 123

Scene 1 London. A gallery in the palace.

Scene 2 Before the council-chamber. Pursuivants, Pages, &c.

Scene 3 The Council-Chamber.

Scene 4 The palace yard.

Scene 5 The palace.

Characters

Anne Bullen (Katharine's maid of honor, afterwards Queen)

Archbishop Cranmer (Archbishop of Canterbury)

Bishop Lincoln

Both

Brandon

Capucius (Ambassador from the Emperor Charles V)

Cardinal Campeius

Cardinal Wolsey

Chorus

Crier

Cromwell (Servant to Wolsey)

Doctor Butts (Physician to the King)

Duke of Buckingham

Duke of Norfolk

Duke of Suffolk

Earl of Surrey

First Gentleman

First Secretary (To Wolsey)

Gardiner (Bishop of Winchester)

Garter (King-at-Arms)

Gentleman

Griffith (Gentleman-usher to Queen Katherine)

Henry VIII

Keeper

Lord Abergavenny

Lord Chamberlain

Lord Chancellor

Lord Sands

Man (The Porter's man)

Messenger

Old Lady (Friend to Anne Bullen)

Page (A page to Gardiner)

Patience (woman to Queen Katharine)

Porter (Door-keeper of the Council-chamber)

Queen Katharine (Wife to King Henry, afterwards divorced)

Scribe

Second Gentleman

Second Secretary (To Wolsey)

Sergeant (A sergeant-at-arms)

Servant

Sir Anthony Denny

Sir Henry Guildford

Sir Nicholas Vaux

Sir Thomas Lovell

Surveyor (To the Duke of Buckingham)

Third Gentleman

Intro

Chorus: I come no more to make you laugh.

Things now that bear a weighty and a serious brow, sad, high, and working full of state and woe, we now present such noble scenes as to draw the eye to flow.

Those that can pity here may, if they think it well, let fall a tear; the subject will deserve it.

Such as give their money out of hope, that they may believe, may here find truth too.

Those that come to see only a show or two, and so agree the play may pass if they be still and willing; I'll undertake may see away their shilling richly in two short hours.

Only they that come to hear a merry bawdy play, a noise of targets, or to see a fellow in a long motley coat guarded with yellow will be deceived; for gentle hearers know to rank our chosen truth with such a show as fool and fight is.

Beside forfeiting our own brains, and the opinion that we bring to make that only true we now intend, will leave us never an understanding friend.

Therefore, for goodness' sake, and as you are known the first and happiest hearers of the town be sad, as we would make ye think ye see the very persons of our noble story as they were living.

Think you see them great and followed with the general throng and sweat of thousand friends, then in a moment see how soon this mightiness meets misery.

If you can be merry then, I'll say a man may weep upon his wedding-day.

Act I, Scene 1

An ante-chamber in the palace. (London)

(Norfolk enters at one door, at the other door Buckingham and Abergavenny)

Duke of Buckingham: Good morrow, and well met. How have ye done since last we saw in France?

Duke of Norfolk: I thank your grace, healthful; and ever since a fresh admirer of what I saw there.

Duke of Buckingham: An untimely ague stayed me a prisoner in my chamber when those suns of glory, those two lights of men, met in the vale of Andren.

Duke of Norfolk: It twist Guynes and Arde.

I was then present, saw them salute on horseback, beheld them when they lighted, how they clung in their embracement as they grew together; which had they, what four throned ones could have weighed, such a compounded one?

Duke of Buckingham: All the whole time I was my chamber's prisoner.

Duke of Norfolk: Then you lost the view of earthly glory.

Men might say till this time pomp was single, but now married to one above itself.

Each following day became the next day's master, till the last made former wonders its.

To-day the French, all clinquant, all in gold like heathen gods, shone down the English; and to-morrow they made Britain India.

Every man that stood showed like a mine, their dwarfish pages were as cherubins, all guilt; the madams too.

Not used to toil, did almost sweat to bear the pride upon them, that their very labour was to them as a painting.

Now this masque was cried incomparable, and the ensuing night made it a fool and beggar.

The two kings, Equal in lustre, were now best, now worst as presence did present them; him in eye still him in praise.

Being present both it was said they saw but one, and no discerner durst wag his tongue in censure.

When these suns, for so they phrase them, by their heralds challenged the noble spirits to arms, they did perform beyond thought's compass that former fabulous story, being now seen possible enough, got credit that Bevis was believed.

Duke of Buckingham: Oh you go far.

Duke of Norfolk: As I belong to worship and affect in honour honesty, the tract of everything would by a good discourser lose some life, which action's self was tongue to; all was royal, to the disposing of it nought rebelled.

Order gave each thing view; the office did distinctly his full function.

Duke of Buckingham: Who did guide, I mean who set the body and the limbs of this great sport together, as you guess?

Duke of Norfolk: One certes that promises no element in such a business.

Duke of Buckingham: I pray you, who, my lord?

Duke of Norfolk: All this was ordered by the good discretion of the right reverend Cardinal of York.

Duke of Buckingham: The devil speed him! no man's pie is freed from his ambitious finger.

What had he to do in these fierce vanities? I wonder that such a keech can with his very bulk, take up the rays of the beneficial sun and keep it from the earth.

Duke of Norfolk: Surely sir, there's in him stuff that puts him to these ends; for, being not propped by ancestry, whose grace chalks successors their way, nor called upon for high feats done to the crown, neither allied for eminent assistants.

Spider-like out of his self-drawing web, he gives us note the force of his own merit makes his way a gift that heaven gives for him, which buys a place next to the king.

Lord Abergavenny: I cannot tell what heaven hath given him, let some graver eye pierce into that, but I can see his pride peep through each part of him.

Whence has he that, if not from hell? The devil is a negligent abuser, or has given all before, and he begins a new hell in himself.

Duke of Buckingham: Why the devil, upon this French going out, took he upon him without the privity of the king; to appoint who should attend on him?

He makes up the file of all the gentry, for the most part such to whom as great a charge as little honour, he meant to lay upon.

His own letter, the honourable board of council out, must fetch him in the papers.

Lord Abergavenny: I do know Kinsmen of mine, three at the least that have by this so sickened their estates, that never they shall abound as formerly.

Duke of Buckingham: Oh many have broke their backs with laying manors on them for this great journey.

What did this vanity but minister communication of a most poor issue?

Duke of Norfolk: Grievingly I think, the peace between the French and us not values the cost that did conclude it.

Duke of Buckingham: Every man brok, after the hideous storm that followed.

Was a thing inspired and not consulting into a general prophecy, that this tempest, dashing the garment of this peace, aboded the sudden breach on't.

Duke of Norfolk: Which is budded out for France hath flawed the league, and hath attached our merchants' goods at Bourdeaux.

Lord Abergavenny: Is it therefore the ambassador is silenced?

Duke of Norfolk: Merrily, is it.

Lord Abergavenny: A proper title of a peace and purchased at a superfluous rate!

Duke of Buckingham: Why, all this business our reverend cardinal carried.

Duke of Norfolk: Like it your grace, the state takes notice of the private difference between you and the cardinal.

I advise you, take it from a heart that wishes towards you honour and plenteous safety; that you read the cardinal's malice and his potency together to consider further that what his high hatred would affect, wanting not a minister in his power.

You know his nature, that he's revengeful, and I know his sword hath a sharp edge.

It's long, and it may be said it reaches far, and where it will not extend thither he darts it.

Bosom up my counsel, you'll find it wholesome.

Lord, where comes that rock that I advise your shunning.

(Cardinal Wolsey enters the purse borne before him certain of the Guard, and two Secretaries with papers.

(Cardinal Wolsey in his passage fixeth his eye on Buckingham, and Buckingham on him, both full of disdain)

Cardinal Wolsey: The Duke of Buckingham's surveyor, ha? Where's his examination?

First Secretary: Here, so please you.

Cardinal Wolsey: Is he in person ready?

First Secretary: Ay, please your grace.

Cardinal Wolsey: Well, we shall then know more; and Buckingham shall lessen this big look.

(Exeunt Cardinal Wolsey and his Train)

Duke of Buckingham: This butcher's cur is venom-mouthed, and I have not the power to muzzle him; therefore best not wake him in his slumber.

A beggar's book outworths a noble's blood.

Duke of Norfolk: What, are you chafed?

Ask God for temperance; that's the appliance only which your disease requires.

Duke of Buckingham: I read in his looks, matter against me; and his eye reviled me, as his abject object: at this instant he bores me with some trick.

He's gone to the king, I'll follow and outstare him.

Duke of Norfolk: Stay my lord, and let your reason with your choler question what it is you go about.

To climb steep hills requires slow pace at first.

Anger is like a full-hot horse, who being allowed his way, self-mettle tires him.

Not a man in England can advise me like you, be to yourself as you would to your friend.

Duke of Buckingham: I'll to the king, and from a mouth of honour quite cry down this Ipswich fellow's insolence; or proclaim there's difference in no persons.

Duke of Norfolk: Be advised, heat not a furnace for your foe so hot that it do singe yourself; we may outrun, by violent swiftness, that which we run at and lose by over-running.

Know you not the fire that mounts the liquor till run over in seeming to augment it wastes it?

Be advised, I say again there is no English soul more stronger to direct you than yourself, if with the sap of reason you would quench, or but allay the fire of passion.

Duke of Buckingham: Sir, I am thankful to you, and I'll go along by your prescription.

This top-proud fellow whom from the flow of gall I name not, but from sincere motions by intelligence and proofs as clear as founts in

July; when we see each grain of gravel I do know to be corrupt and treasonous.

Duke of Norfolk: Say not treasonous.

Duke of Buckingham: To the king I'll say it and make my vouch as strong as shore of rock.

Attend this holy fox or wolf, or both, for he is equal ravenous as he is subtle, and as prone to mischief as able to perform it; his mind and place infecting one another, yea, reciprocally…

Only to show his pomp as well in France as here at home, suggests the king our master to this last costly treaty; the interview that swallowed so much treasure and like a glass did break in the rinsing.

Duke of Norfolk: Faith, and so it did.

Duke of Buckingham: Pray, give me favour sir.

This cunning cardinal, the articles of the combination drew as himself pleased, and they were ratified as he cried: Thus let be, to as much end

As give a crutch to the dead, but our count-cardinal has done this, and 'tis well; for worthy Wolsey, who cannot err, he did it. Now this follows…

Which as I take it, is a kind of puppy to the old dam, treason, Charles the emperor, under pretence to see the queen his aunt…

For it was indeed his colour, but he came to whisper Wolsey, here makes visitation.

His fears were, that the interview between England and France might, through their amity breed him some prejudice, for from this league peeped harms that menaced him.

He privily deals with our cardinal, and as I throw, which I do well, for I am sure the emperor paid were he promised; whereby his suit was granted were it was asked, but when the way was made and paved with gold the emperor thus desired that he would please to alter the king's course, and break the foresaid peace.

Let the king know, as soon he shall by me, that thus the cardinal does buy and sell his honour as he pleases, and for his own advantage.

Duke of Norfolk: I am sorry to hear this of him and could wish he were something mistaken in it.

Duke of Buckingham: No, not a syllable, I do pronounce him in that very shape he shall appear in proof.

(Brandon enters with a Sergeant-at-arms before him, and two or three of the Guard)

Brandon: Your office, sergeant; execute it.

Sergeant: Sir, my lord the Duke of Buckingham, and Earl of Hereford, Stafford, and Northampton, arrest thee of high treason, in the name of our most sovereign king.

Duke of Buckingham: Lord, you my lord, the net has fallen upon me!

I shall perish under device and practise.

Brandon: I am sorry to see you taken from liberty, to look on the business present.

It is his highness' pleasure, you shall to the Tower.

Duke of Buckingham: It will help me nothing to plead mine innocence for that dye is on me which makes my whitest part black.

The will of heaven be done in this and all things! I obey.

Oh my Lord Abergavenny, fare you well!

Brandon: Nay, he must bear you company. The king 290

(To **Abergavenny**)

Is pleased you shall to the Tower, till you know

How he determines further.

Lord Abergavenny: As the duke said, the will of heaven be done and the king's pleasure by me obeyed!

Brandon: Here is a warrant from the king to attach Lord Montacute, and the bodies of the duke's confessor, John de la Car, one Gilbert Peck his chancellor.

Duke of Buckingham: So, so, these are the limbs of the plot.

No more, I hope.

Brandon: A monk of the Chartreux.

Duke of Buckingham: Oh Nicholas Hopkins?

Brandon: He.

Duke of Buckingham: My surveyor is false, the over-great cardinal hath showed him gold; my life is spanned already.

I am the shadow of poor Buckingham, whose figure even this instant cloud puts on by darkening my clear sun.

My lord, farewell.

(Exeunt)

Act I, Scene 2

The council-chamber.

(Cornets)

(King Henry VIII enters leaning on Cardinal Wolsey's shoulder, the Nobles, and Lovell)

(Cardinal Wolsey places himself under King Henry VIII's feet on his right side)

Henry VIII: My life itself, and the best heart of it; thanks you for this great care.

I stood in the level of a full-charged confederacy, and give thanks to you that choked it.

Let be called before us that gentleman of Buckingham's in person, I'll hear him his confessions justify; and point by point the treasons of his master he shall again relate.

(A noise within crying: Room for the Queen!')

(Queen Katharine enters ushered by Norfolk, and Suffolk kneels)

(King Henry VIII riseth from his state, takes her up, kisses and placeth her by him)

Queen Katharine: Nay, we must longer kneel: I am a suitor.

Henry VIII: Arise, and take place by us.

Half your suit never name to us, you have half our power.

The other moiety, ere you ask, is given; repeat your will and take it.

Queen Katharine: Thank your majesty.

That you would love yourself, and in that love not unconsidered leave your honour, nor the dignity of your office, is the point of my petition.

Henry VIII: Lady mine, proceed.

Queen Katharine: I am solicited, not by a few, and those of true condition that your subjects are in great grievance.

There have been commissions sent down among them, which hath flawed the heart of all their loyalties wherein; although my good lord cardinal, they vent reproaches most bitterly on you, as putter on of these exactions, yet the king our master…

Whose honour heaven shield from soil! Even he escapes not language unmannerly, yea, such which breaks the sides of loyalty, and almost appears in loud rebellion.

Duke of Norfolk: Not almost appears, it doth appear for upon these taxations, the clothiers all; not able to maintain the many to them longing have put off the spinsters, carders, fullers, weavers, who unfit for other life are compelled by hunger and lack of other means.

In desperate manner daring the event to the teeth are all in uproar, and danger serves among then!

Henry VIII: Taxation!

Wherein? and what taxation? My lord cardinal, you that are blamed for it alike with us, know you of this taxation?

Cardinal Wolsey: Please you, sir, I know but of a single part, in aught, pertains to the state; and front but in that file where others tell steps with me.

Queen Katharine: No, my lord, you know no more than others; but you frame things that are known alike; which are not wholesome to those which would not know them, and yet must perforce be their acquaintance.

These exactions, whereof my sovereign would have note, they are most pestilent to the bearing, and to bear them.

The back is sacrifice to the load; they say they are devised by you, or else you suffer too hard an exclamation.

Henry VIII: Still exaction!

The nature of it? In what kind, let's know, is this exaction?

Queen Katharine: I am much too venturous in tempting of your patience, but am boldened under your promised pardon.

The subjects' grief comes through commissions, which compel from each the sixth part of his substance, to be levied without delay; and the pretence for this is named your wars in France.

This makes bold mouths, tongues spit their duties out, and cold hearts freeze allegiance in them; their curses now live where their prayers did; and it's come to pass.

This tractable obedience is a slave, to each incensed will.

I would your highness would give it quick consideration, for there is no primer business.

Henry VIII: By my life, this is against our pleasure.

Cardinal Wolsey: And for me, I have no further gone in this than by a single voice; and that not passed me, but by learned approbation of the judges.

If I am traduced by ignorant tongues, which neither know my faculties nor person, yet will be the chronicles of my doing; let me say it is but the fate of place, and the rough brake that virtue must go through.

We must not stint our necessary actions, in the fear to cope malicious censurers, which ever as ravenous fishes do a vessel follow that is new-trimmed, but benefit no further than vainly longing.

What we oft do best, by sick interpreters, once weak ones is not ours, or not allowed; what worst, as often hitting a grosser quality is cried up for our best act.

If we shall stand still, in fear our motion will be mocked or carped at, we should take root here where we sit, or sit state-statues only.

Henry VIII: Things done well, and with a care exempt themselves from fear; things done without example, in their issue are to be feared.

Have you a precedent of this commission? I believe, not any.

We must not rend our subjects from our laws, and stick them in our will.

Sixth part of each? A trembling contribution! Why, we take from every tree lop, bark, and part of the timber; and though we leave it with a root, thus hacked the air will drink the sap.

To every county where this is questioned send our letters, with free pardon to each man that has denied the force of this commission.

Pray, look to it, I put it to your care.

Cardinal Wolsey: A word with you.

(To the Secretary)

Let there be letters writ to every shire, of the king's grace and pardon.

The grieved commons hardly conceive of me, let it be noised that through our intercession this revokement and pardon comes.

I shall anon advise you further in the proceeding.

(Secretary exits)

(Surveyor enters)

Queen Katharine: I am sorry that the Duke of Buckingham is run in your displeasure.

Henry VIII: It grieves many, the gentleman is learned and a most rare speaker to nature none more bound; his training such that he may furnish and instruct great teachers and never seek for aid out of himself.

Yet see, when these so noble benefits shall prove not well disposed, the mind growing once corrupt they turn to vicious forms, ten times more ugly than ever they were fair.

This man so complete who was enrolled 'mongst wonders, and when we almost with ravished listening, could not find his hour of speech a minute; he my lady, hath into monstrous habits put the graces that once were his, and is become as black as if besmeared in hell.

Sit by us, you shall hear, This was his gentleman in trust of him things to strike honour sad.

Bid him recount the fore-recited practises; whereof we cannot feel too little, hear too much.

Cardinal Wolsey: Stand forth, and with bold spirit relate what you, most like a careful subject have collected out of the Duke of Buckingham.

Henry VIII: Speak freely.

Surveyor: First, it was usual with him, every day it would infect his speech, that if the king should without issue die; he'll carry it so to make the sceptre his.

These very words I've heard him utter to his son-in-law, Lord Abergavenny, to whom by oath he menaced revenge upon the cardinal.

Cardinal Wolsey: Please your highness, note this dangerous conception in this point.

Not friended by his wish, to your high person his will is most malignant; and it stretches beyond you to your friends.

Queen Katharine: My learn'd lord cardinal, deliver all with charity.

Henry VIII: Speak on, how grounded he his title to the crown, upon our fail?

To this point hast thou heard him at any time speak aught?

Surveyor: He was brought to this by a vain prophecy of Nicholas Hopkins.

Henry VIII: What was that Hopkins?

Surveyor: Sir, a Chartreux friar, his confessor, who fed him every minute with words of sovereignty.

Henry VIII: How know'st thou this?

Surveyor: Not long before your highness sped to France,

The duke being at the Rose, within the parish Saint Lawrence Poultney, did of me demand what was the speech among the Londoners, concerning the French journey.

I replied, men feared the French would prove perfidious, to the king's danger.

Presently the duke said it was the fear, indeed, and that he doubted it would prove the verity of certain words spoke by a holy monk; that often says he hath sent to me, wishing me to permit John de la Car, my chaplain, a choice hour, to hear from him a matter of some moment.

Whom after under the confession's seal he solemnly had sworn, that what he spoke my chaplain to no creature living, but to me should utter with demure confidence, this pausingly ensued.

Neither the king nor his heirs tell you the duke, shall prosper.

Bid him strive to gain the love of the commonalty.

The duke shall govern England.

Queen Katharine: If I know you well, you were the duke's surveyor, and lost your office on the complaint o' the tenants.

Take good heed, you charge not in your spleen a noble person and spoil your nobler soul.

I say take heed, yes, heartily beseech you.

Henry VIII: Let him on.

Go forward.

Surveyor: On my soul, I'll speak but truth.

I told my lord the duke, by the devil's illusions the monk might be deceived, and that it was dangerous for him to ruminate on this so far; until It forged him some design, which, being believed it was much like to do.

He answered: Tush, it can do me no damage, adding further, that had the king in his last sickness failed, the cardinal's and Sir Thomas Lovell's heads should have gone off.

Henry VIII: Ha! what, so rank? Ah ha!

There's mischief in this man: canst thou say further?

Surveyor: I can, my liege.

Henry VIII: Proceed.

Surveyor: Being at Greenwich, after your highness had reproved the duke about Sir William Blomer...

Henry VIII: I remember of such a time: being my sworn servant, the duke retained him his, but on what hence?

Surveyor: If, quoth he, I for this had been committed, as to the Tower; I thought, I would have played the part my father meant to act upon the usurper Richard.

Richard, who being at Salisbury made suit to come in's presence, which if granted as he made semblance of his duty, would have put his knife to him.

Henry VIII: A giant traitor!

Cardinal Wolsey: Now madam, may his highness live in freedom, and this man out of prison?

Queen Katharine: God mend all!

Henry VIII: There's something more would out of thee; what say'st?

Surveyor: After the duke his father, with the knife he stretched him, and with one hand on his dagger, another spread on his breast mounting his eyes; he did discharge a horrible oath, whose tenor was…

Were he evil used, he would outgo his father by as much as a performance does an irresolute purpose.

Henry VIII: There's his period, to sheathe his knife in us.

He is attached, call him to present trial.

If he may find mercy in the law, it is his.

If none, let him not seek it of us, by day and night he's traitor to the height.

(Exeunt)

Act I, Scene 3

An ante-chamber in the palace.

(Chamberlain and Sands enter)

Lord Chamberlain: Is it possible the spells of France should juggle men into such strange mysteries?

Lord Sands: New customs, though they be never so ridiculous; nay, let them be unmanly, yet are followed.

Lord Chamberlain: As far as I see, all the good our English have got by the late voyage is, but merely a fit or two on the face; but they are shrewd ones for when they hold them, you would swear directly their very noses had been counsellors to Pepin or Clotharius, they keep state so.

Lord Sands: They have all new legs, and lame ones: one would take it, that never saw them pace before, the spavin or springhalt reigned among them.

Lord Chamberlain: Death! My lord, their clothes are after such a pagan cut too; that, sure they've worn out Christendom.

(Lovell enters)

How now!

What news, Sir Thomas Lovell?

Sir Thomas Lovell: Faith, my lord, I hear of none, but the new proclamation that's clapped upon the court-gate.

Lord Chamberlain: What is it for?

Sir Thomas Lovell: The reformation of our travelled gallants that fill the court with quarrels, talk, and tailors.

Lord Chamberlain: I'm glad 'tis there: now I would pray our monsieurs to think an English courtier may be wise, and never see the Louvre.

Sir Thomas Lovell: They must either, for so run the conditions, leave those remnants of fool and feather that they got in France, with all their honourable point of ignorance pertaining thereunto, as fights and fireworks, abusing better men than they can be.

Out of a foreign wisdom, renouncing clean the faith they have in tennis, and tall stockings short blistered breeches, and those types of travel, and understand again like honest men; or pack to their old playfellows.

There, I take it they may cum privilegio, wear away the lag end of their lewdness and be laughed at.

Lord Sands: It is time to give them physic, their diseases are grown so catching.

Lord Chamberlain: What a loss our ladies

Will have of these trim vanities!

Sir Thomas Lovell: Ay, marry, there will be woe indeed lords.

The sly whoresons have got a speeding trick to lay down ladies, a French song and a fiddle has no fellow.

Lord Sands: The devil fiddle them! I am glad they are going, for sure there's no converting of them.

Now an honest country lord, as I am, beaten a long time out of play may bring his plainsong and have an hour of hearing; and by'r lady held current music too.

Lord Chamberlain: Well said, Lord Sands, your colt's tooth is not cast yet.

Lord Sands: No, my lord, nor shall not, while I have a stump.

Lord Chamberlain: Sir Thomas, whither were you a-going?

Sir Thomas Lovell: To the cardinal's.

Your lordship is a guest too.

Lord Chamberlain: Oh, it is true.

This night he makes a supper, and a great one, to many lords and ladies; there will be the beauty of this kingdom, I'll assure you.

Sir Thomas Lovell: That churchman bears a bounteous mind indeed, a hand as fruitful as the land that feeds us; his dews fall everywhere.

Lord Chamberlain: No doubt he's noble; he had a black mouth that said other of him.

Lord Sands: He may, my lord; has wherewithal: in him

Sparing would show a worse sin than ill doctrine, Men of his way should be most liberal; they are set here for examples.

Lord Chamberlain: True, they are so, but few now give so great ones.

My barge stays, your lordship shall along.

Come, good Sir Thomas, we shall be late else; which I would not be, for I was spoke to, with Sir Henry Guildford this night to be comptrollers.

Lord Sands: I am your lordship's.

(Exeunt)

Act I, Scene 4

A Hall in York Place.

(A small table under a state for Cardinal Wolsey, a longer table for the guests)

(Anne enters and divers other Ladies and Gentlemen as guests, at one door; at another door, enter Guildford)

Sir Henry Guildford: Ladies, a general welcome from his grace salutes ye all, this night he dedicates to fair content and you; none here he hopes in all this noble bevy, has brought with her one care abroad, he would have all as merry.

As first good company, good wine, good welcome can make good people.

Oh my lord, you're tardy.

(Chamberlain, Sands, and Lovell enter)

The very thought of this fair company clapped wings to me.

Lord Chamberlain: You are young, Sir Harry Guildford.

Lord Sands: Sir Thomas Lovell, had the cardinal but half my lay thoughts in him, some of these should find a running banquet were they rested; I think would better please them.

By my life, they are a sweet society of fair ones.

Sir Thomas Lovell: Oh that your lordship were but now confessor to one or two of these!

Lord Sands: I would I were, they should find easy penance.

Sir Thomas Lovell: Faith, how easy?

Lord Sands: As easy as a down-bed would afford it.

Lord Chamberlain: Sweet ladies, will it please you sit? Sir Harry, place you that side; I'll take the charge of this.

His grace is entering, nay, you must not freeze two women placed together makes cold weather.

My Lord Sands, you are one will keep them waking; pray, sit between these ladies.

Lord Sands: By my faith, and thank your lordship.

By your leave sweet ladies; if I chance to talk a little wild, forgive me I had it from my father.

Anne Bullen: Was he mad, sir?

Lord Sands: Oh very mad exceeding mad, in love too, but he would bite none; just as I do now, he would kiss you twenty with a breath.

(Kisses her)

Lord Chamberlain: Well said, my lord.

So, now you're fairly seated.

Gentlemen, the penance lies on you, if these fair ladies pass away frowning.

Lord Sands: For my little cure, let me alone.

(Cardinal Wolsey enters)

Cardinal Wolsey: You're welcome, my fair guests that noble lady, or gentleman that is not freely merry; is not my friend.

This, to confirm my welcome and to you all, good health.

(Drinks)

Lord Sands: Your grace is noble, let me have such a bowl may hold my thanks, and save me so much talking.

Cardinal Wolsey: My Lord Sands, I am beholding to you: cheer your neighbours.

Ladies, you are not merry; gentlemen whose fault is this?

Lord Sands: The red wine first must rise in their fair cheeks, my lord, then we shall have them.

Talk us to silence.

Anne Bullen: You are a merry gamester my Lord Sands.

Lord Sands: Yes, if I make my play.

Here's to your ladyship, and pledge it, madam, for it is to such a thing…

Anne Bullen: You cannot show me.

Lord Sands: I told your grace they would talk ah no.

(Drum and trumpet, chambers discharged)

Cardinal Wolsey: What's that?

Lord Chamberlain: Look out there, some of ye.

(Exit Servant)

Cardinal Wolsey: What warlike voice, and to what end is this?

Nay, ladies, fear not by all the laws of war you're privileged.

(Servant re-enters)

Lord Chamberlain: How now! What is it?

Servant: A noble troop of strangers, for so they seem.

They've left their barge and landed, and hither make, as great ambassadors from foreign princes.

Cardinal Wolsey: Good lord chamberlain, go give them welcome; you can speak the French tongue, and pray, receive them nobly, and conduct them into our presence where this heaven of beauty shall shine at full upon them.

Some attend him.

(Chamberlain exits attended)

(All rise, and tables are removed)

You have now a broken banquet, but we'll mend it.

A good digestion to you all, and once more I shower a welcome on ye, welcome all.

(King Henry VIII and others enter as masquers, habited like shepherds, ushered by the Chamberlain)

(They pass directly before Cardinal Wolsey and gracefully salute him)

A noble company! What are their pleasures?

Lord Chamberlain: Because they speak no English, thus they prayed to tell your grace, that, having heard by fame of this so noble, and so fair assembly this night to meet here.

They could do no less out of the great respect they bear to beauty, but leave their flocks; and, under your fair conduct, crave leave to view these ladies and entreat an hour of revels with them.

Cardinal Wolsey: Say, lord chamberlain, they have done my poor house grace; for which I pay them a thousand thanks, and pray them take their pleasures.

(They choose Ladies for the dance)

(King Henry chooses Anne)

Henry VIII: The fairest hand I ever touched! Oh beauty, till now I never knew thee!

(Music, Dance)

Cardinal Wolsey: My lord!

Lord Chamberlain: Your grace?

Cardinal Wolsey: Pray, tell them thus much from me.

There should be one amongst them, by his person, more worthy this place than myself; to whom, if I but knew him with my love and duty I would surrender it.

Lord Chamberlain: I will, my lord.

(The Masquers whispers)

Cardinal Wolsey: What say they?

Lord Chamberlain: Such a one, they all confess, there is indeed, which they would have your grace.

Find out, and he will take it.

Cardinal Wolsey: Let me see, then.

By all your good leaves, gentlemen, here I'll make my royal choice.

Henry VIII: Ye have found him, cardinal:

(Unmasking)

You hold a fair assembly, you do well lord.

You are a churchman, or, I'll tell you cardinal, I should judge now unhappily.

Cardinal Wolsey: I am glad your grace is grown so pleasant.

Henry VIII: My lord chamberlain, pray to thee, come hither.

What fair lady's that?

Lord Chamberlain: And if it please your grace, Sir Thomas Bullen's daughter...

The Viscount Rochford, one of her highness' women.

Henry VIII: By heaven, she is a dainty one.

Sweetheart, I were unmannerly to take you out and not to kiss you.

A health, gentlemen! Let it go round.

Cardinal Wolsey: Sir Thomas Lovell, is the banquet ready in the privy chamber?

Sir Thomas Lovell: Yes, my lord.

Cardinal Wolsey: Your grace, I fear with dancing is a little heated.

Henry VIII: I fear, too much.

Cardinal Wolsey: There's fresher air, my lord, in the next chamber.

Henry VIII: Lead in your ladies, every one.

Sweet partner, I must not yet forsake you, let's be merry.

Good my lord cardinal, I have half a dozen healths to drink to these fair ladies, and a measure to lead them once again; and then let's dream who's best in favour.

Let the music knock it.

(Exeunt with trumpets)

Act II, Scene 1

A street. (Westminster)

(Two Gentlemen enter, meeting)

First Gentleman: Whither away so fast?

Second Gentleman: Oh God save ye!

Even to the hall, to hear what shall become of the great Duke of Buckingham.

First Gentleman: I'll save you that labour, sir. all's now done but the ceremony of bringing back the prisoner.

Second Gentleman: Were you there?

First Gentleman: Yes, indeed, was I.

Second Gentleman: Pray, speak what has happened.

First Gentleman: You may guess quickly what.

Second Gentleman: Is he found guilty?

First Gentleman: Yes, truly is he, and condemned upon it.

Second **Gentleman:** I am sorry for it.

First Gentleman: So are a number more.

Second **Gentleman:** But, pray, how passed it?

First Gentleman: I'll tell you in a little.

The great duke came to the bar where to his accusations, he pleaded still not guilty and alleged many sharp reasons to defeat the law.

The king's attorney on the contrary urged on the examinations, proofs, confessions of divers witnesses; which the duke desired to have brought viva voce to his face.

At which appeared against him his surveyor, Sir Gilbert Peck his chancellor, and John Car, confessor to him with that devil-monk, Hopkins, that made this mischief.

Second Gentleman: That was he That fed him with his prophecies?

First Gentleman: The same.

All these accused him strongly, which he fain would have flung from him, but indeed he could not; and so his peers, upon this evidence,

Have found him guilty of high treason.

Much he spoke, and learnedly, for life, but all was either pitied in him or forgotten.

Second Gentleman: After all this, how did he bear himself?

First Gentleman: When he was brought again to the bar, to hear his knell rung out, his judgment, he was stirred with such an agony, he sweat extremely, and something spoke in choler, ill, and hasty.

He fell to himself again, and sweetly in all the rest showed a most noble patience.

Second Gentleman: I do not think he fears death.

First Gentleman: Sure, he does not.

He never was so womanish, the cause he may a little grieve at.

Second Gentleman: Certainly the cardinal is the end of this.

First Gentleman: It is likely, by all conjectures.

First, Kildare's attainder, then deputy of Ireland; who removed Earl Surrey, was sent thither and in haste too, lest he should help his father.

Second Gentleman: That trick of state was a deep envious one.

First Gentleman: At his return no doubt he will requite it.

This is noted, and generally, whoever the king favours the cardinal instantly will find employment and far enough from court too.

Second Gentleman: All the commons hate him perniciously, and, of my conscience, wish him ten fathom deep.

This duke as much they love and dote on, call him bounteous Buckingham, the mirror of all courtesy…

First Gentleman: Stay there, sir, and see the noble ruined man you speak of.

(Buckingham enters from his arraignment, tip-staves are before him; the axe with the edge towards him halberds on each side, accompanied with Lovell, Vaux, Sands, and common people)

Second Gentleman: Let's stand close, and behold him.

Duke of Buckingham: All good people, you that thus far have come to pity me, hear what I say, and then go home and lose me.

I have this day received a traitor's judgment, and by that name must die.

Yet, heaven bear witness and if I have a conscience, let it sink me, even as the axe falls if I be not faithful!

The law I bear no malice for my death, it has done upon the premises, but justice, but those that sought it I could wish more Christians.

Be what they will, I heartily forgive them, yet let them look they glory not in mischief; nor build their evils on the graves of great men for then my guiltless blood must cry against them.

For further life in this world I ne'er hope, nor will I sue, although the king have mercies more than I dare make faults.

You few that loved me, and dare be bold to weep for Buckingham; his noble friends and fellows, whom to leave is only bitter to him, only dying.

Go with me, like good angels, to my end, and as the long divorce of steel falls on me; make of your prayers one sweet sacrifice and lift my soul to heaven.

Lead on, of God's name.

Sir Thomas Lovell: I do beseech your grace, for charity, if ever any malice in your heart were hid against me, now to forgive me frankly.

Duke of Buckingham: Sir Thomas Lovell, I as free forgive you as I would be forgiven.

I forgive all, there cannot be those numberless offences against me, that I cannot take peace with.

No black envy shall mark my grave.

Commend me to his grace, and if he speak of Buckingham, pray, tell him you met him half in heaven.

My vows and prayers yet are the king's, and till my soul forsake shall cry for blessings on him.

May he live longer than I have time to tell his years!

Ever beloved and loving may his rule be!

And when old time shall lead him to his end, goodness and he fill up one monument!

Sir Thomas Lovell: To the water side I must conduct your grace, then give my charge up to Sir Nicholas Vaux, who undertakes you to your end.

Sir Nicholas Vaux: Prepare there, the duke is coming: see the barge be ready; and fit it with such furniture as suits the greatness of his person.

Duke of Buckingham: Nay, Sir Nicholas, let it alone; my state now will but mock me.

When I came hither, I was lord high constable, and Duke of Buckingham; now, poor Edward Bohun.

Yet I am richer than my base accusers, that never knew what truth meant.

I now seal it, and with that blood will make them one day groan for it.

My noble father, Henry of Buckingham, who first raised head against usurping Richard, flying for succor to his servant Banister, being distressed was by that wretch betrayed, and without trial fell.

God's peace be with him!

Henry the Seventh succeeding, truly pitying my father's loss, like a most royal prince, restored me to my honours, and, out of ruins made my name once more noble.

Now his son, Henry the Eighth, life, honour, name and all that made me happy at one stroke has taken for ever from the world. I had my trial, and must needs say a noble one; which makes me, a little happier than my wretched father.

Yet thus far we are one in fortunes.

Both fell by our servants by those men we loved most, a most unnatural and faithless service! Heaven has an end in all.

Yet, you that hear me, this from a dying man receive as certain.

Where you are liberal of your loves and counsels be sure you be not loose, for those you make friends, and give your hearts to when they once perceive the least rub in your fortunes, fall away like water from ye, never found again but where they mean to sink ye.

All good people, pray for me! I must now forsake ye.

The last hour of my long weary life is come upon me.

Farewell.

And when you would say something that is sad, speak how I fell.

I have done; and God forgive me!

(Exeunt Buckingham and Train)

First Gentleman: Oh this is full of pity! Sir it calls, I fear, too many curses on their beads that were the authors.

Second Gentleman: If the duke be guiltless, it is full of woe.

Yet I can give you inkling of an ensuing evil, if it fall, greater than this.

First Gentleman: Good angels keep it from us!

What may it be? You do not doubt my faith, sir?

Second Gentleman: This secret is so weighty, it will require a strong faith to conceal it.

First Gentleman: Let me have it, I do not talk much.

Second Gentleman: I am confident, you shall sir; did you not of late days hear a buzzing of a separation between the king and Katharine?

First Gentleman: Yes, but it held not, for when the king once heard it, out of anger he sent command to the lord mayor straight to stop the rumor, and allay those tongues that durst disperse it.

Second Gentleman: But that slander sir, is found a truth now; for it grows again fresher than ever it was, and held for certain the king will venture at it.

Either the cardinal, or some about him near, have, out of malice to the good queen possessed him with a scruple that will undo her.

To confirm this too, Cardinal Campeius is arrived, and lately as all think, for this business.

First Gentleman: It is the cardinal, and merely to revenge him on the emperor for not bestowing on him, at his asking the archbishopric of Toledo, this is purposed.

Second Gentleman: I think you have hit the mark, but is it not cruel that she should feel the smart of this?

The cardinal will have his will, and she must fall.

First Gentleman: It is woeful.

We are too open here to argue this, let's think in private more.

(Exeunt)

Act II, Scene 2

An ante-chamber in the palace.

(Chamberlain enters reading a letter)

Lord Chamberlain: My lord, the horses your lordship sent for, with all the care I had, I saw well chosen, ridden, and furnished.

They were young and handsome, and of the best breed in the north.

When they were ready to set out for London, a man of my lord cardinal's, by commission and main power took them from me; with this reason: his master would be served before a subject, if not before the king, which stopped our mouths sir.

I fear he will indeed, well, let him have the.

He will have all, I think.

(Norkfolk and Suffolk enter to Chamberlain)

Duke of Norfolk: Well met, my lord chamberlain.

Lord Chamberlain: Good day to both your graces.

Duke of Suffolk: How is the king employed?

Lord Chamberlain: I left him private, full of sad thoughts and troubles.

Duke of Norfolk: What's the cause?

Lord Chamberlain: It seems the marriage with his brother's wife has crept too near his conscience.

Duke of Suffolk: No, his conscience has crept too near another lady.

Duke of Norfolk: It is so.

This is the cardinal's doing, the king-cardinal that blind priest, like the eldest son of fortune turns what he list.

The king will know him one day.

Duke of Suffolk: Pray God he do! He'll never know himself else.

Duke of Norfolk: How holily he works in all his business! And with what zeal!

For, now he has cracked the league between us and the emperor, the queen's great nephew, He dives into the king's soul, and there scatters dangers, doubts, wringing of the conscience, fears, and despairs; and all these for his marriage.

And out of all these to restore the king, he counsels a divorce; a loss of her that, like a jewel, has hung twenty years about his neck, yet never lost her lustre; of her that loves him with that excellence that angels love good men with.

Even of her that, when the greatest stroke of fortune falls, will bless the king: and is not this course pious?

Lord Chamberlain: Heaven keep me from such counsel! It is most true these news are everywhere; every tongue speaks them and every true heart weeps for it; all that dare look into these affairs see this main end the French king's sister.

Heaven will one day open the king's eyes, that so long have slept upon This bold bad man.

Duke of Suffolk: And free us from his slavery.

Duke of Norfolk: We had need pray, and heartily, for our deliverance; or this imperious man will work us all from princes into pages.

All men's honours lie like one lump before him, to be fashioned into what pitch he please.

Duke of Suffolk: For me, my lords, I love him not, nor fear him; there's my creed.

As I am made without him, so I'll stand, if the king please; his curses and his blessings touch me alike, they're breath I not believe in.

I knew him, and I know him, so I leave him, to him that made him proud, the pope.

Duke of Norfolk: Let's in; and with some other business put the king from these sad thoughts that work too much upon him.

My lord, you'll bear us company?

Lord Chamberlain: Excuse me; the king has sent me otherwhere.

Besides, you'll find a most unfit time to disturb him.

Health to your lordships.

Duke of Norfolk: Thanks, my good lord chamberlain.

(Chamberlain enters and King Henry VIII draws the curtain, and sits reading pensively)

Duke of Suffolk: How sad he looks! Sure, he is much afflicted.

Henry VIII: Who's there, ha?

Duke of Norfolk: Pray God he be not angry.

Henry VIII: Who's there, I say? How dare you thrust yourselves into my private meditations?

Who am I? ha?

Duke of Norfolk: A gracious king that pardons all offences malice ne'er meant, our breach of duty this way is business of estate; in which we come to know your royal pleasure.

Henry VIII: Ye are too bold.

Go to, I'll make ye know your times of business, is this an hour for temporal affairs, ha?

(Cardinal Wolsey and Cardinal Campeius enter with a commission)

Who's there? My good lord cardinal? Oh my Wolsey, the quiet of my wounded conscience; thou art a cure fit for a king.

(To Cardinal Campeius)

You're welcome, most learned reverend sir, into our kingdom.

Use us and it.

(To Cardinal Wolsey)

My good lord, have great care

I be not found a talker.

Cardinal Wolsey: Sir, you cannot.

I would your grace would give us but an hour of private conference.

Henry VIII: (To Norfolk and Suffolk)

We are busy, go.

Duke of Norfolk: (From Aside to Suffolk)

This priest has no pride in him?

Duke of Suffolk: (From Aside to Norfolk) Not to speak of.

I would not be so sick though for his place.

This cannot continue.

Duke of Norfolk: (From Aside to Suffolk) If it do, I'll venture one have-at-him.

Duke of Suffolk: (From Aside to Norfolk) I another.

(Exeunt Norfolk and Suffolk)

Cardinal Wolsey: Your grace has given a precedent of wisdom above all princes, in committing freely your scruple to the voice of Christendom.

Who can be angry now? What envy reach you?

The Spaniard, tied blood and favour to her, must now confess, if they have any goodness, the trial just and noble.

All the clerks, I mean the learned ones in Christian kingdoms, have their free voices.

Rome, the nurse of judgment, invited by your noble self, hath sent one general tongue unto us, this good man, this just and learned priest.

Cardinal Campeius, whom once more I present unto your highness.

Henry VIII: And once more in mine arms I bid him welcome, and thank the holy conclave for their loves.

They have sent me such a man I would have wished for.

Cardinal Campeius: Your grace must needs deserve all strangers' loves, you are so noble.

To your highness' hand I tender my commission, by whose virtue, the court of Rome commanding you, my lord Cardinal of York are joined with me their servant in the unpartial judging of this business.

Henry VIII: Two equal men.

The queen shall be acquainted forthwith for what you come.

Where's Gardiner?

Cardinal Wolsey: I know your majesty has always loved her so dear in heart, not to deny her that a woman of less place might ask by law.

Scholars allowed freely to argue for her.

Henry VIII: Ay, and the best she shall have; and my favour to him that does best, God forbid else.

Cardinal, I pray to the, call Gardiner to me, my new secretary.

I find him a fit fellow.

(Cardinal Wolsey exits)

(Cardinal Wolsey re-enters with Gardiner)

Cardinal Wolsey: (From Aside to Gardiner) Give me your hand much joy and favour to you; you are the king's now.

Gardiner: (From Aside to Cardinal Wolsey)

But to be commanded for ever by your grace, whose hand has raised me.

Henry VIII: Come hither, Gardiner.

(Walks and whispers)

Cardinal Campeius: My Lord of York, was not one Doctor Pace in this man's place before him?

Cardinal Wolsey: Yes, he was.

Cardinal Campeius: Was he not held a learned man?

Cardinal Wolsey: Yes, surely.

Cardinal Campeius: Believe me, there's an ill opinion spread then even of yourself, lord cardinal.

Cardinal Wolsey: How! Of me?

Cardinal Campeius: They will not stick to say you envied him, and fearing he would rise, he was so virtuous, kept him a foreign man still; which so grieved him that he ran mad and died.

Cardinal Wolsey: Heaven's peace be with him! That's Christian care enough.

For living murmurers there's places of rebuke.

He was a fool, for he would needs be virtuous.

That good fellow, if I command him, follows my appointment I will have none so near else; learn this, brother, we live not to be griped by meaner persons.

Henry VIII: Deliver this with modesty to the queen.

(Gardiner exits)

The most convenient place that I can think of for such receipt of learning is Black-Friars; there ye shall meet about this weighty business.

My Wolsey, see it furnished.

Oh my lord, would it not grieve an able man to leave so sweet a bedfellow? But, conscience, conscience!

Oh it is a tender place; and I must leave her.

(Exeunt)

Act II, Scene 3

An ante-chamber of the Queen's apartments.

(Anne and an Old Lady enter)

Anne Bullen: Not for that neither, here's the pang that pinches his highness, having lived so long with her; and she, so good a lady that no tongue could ever pronounce dishonour of her by my life, she never knew harm-doing.

Oh now, after so many courses of the sun enthroned, still growing in a majesty and pomp the which to leave a thousand-fold more bitter than it is sweet at first to acquire; after this process, to give her the forward!

It is a pity, would move a monster.

Old Lady: Hearts of most hard temper melt and lament for her.

Anne Bullen: Oh God's will! Much better, she never had known pomp.

Though it be temporal, yet if that quarrel, fortune, do divorce it from the bearer, it is a sufferance panging; as soul and body's severing.

Old Lady: Alas, poor lady! She's a stranger now again.

Anne Bullen: So much the more, must pity drop upon her.

Verily, I swear, it is better to be lowly born and range with humble livers in content, than to be perked up in a glistering grief and wear a golden sorrow.

Old Lady: Our content is our best having.

Anne Bullen: By my troth and maidenhead, I would not be a queen.

Old Lady: Beshrew me, I would, and venture maidenhead for it; and so would you, for all this spice of your hypocrisy.

You, that have so fair parts of woman on you, have too a woman's heart, whichever yet affected eminence, wealth, sovereignty; which to say sooth, are blessings and which gifts; saving your mincing.

The capacity of your soft cheveril conscience would receive if you might please to stretch it.

Anne Bullen: Nay, good troth.

Old Lady: Yes, troth, and troth; you would not be a queen?

Anne Bullen: No, not for all the riches under heaven.

Old as I am, to queen it, but, I pray you, what think you of a duchess?

Have you limbs to bear that load of title?

Anne Bullen: No, in truth.

Old Lady: Then you are weakly made: pluck off a little, I would not be a young count in your way for more than blushing comes to: if your back cannot vouchsafe this burthen;it is too weak ever to get a boy.

Anne Bullen: How you do talk!

I swear again, I would not be a queen for all the world.

Old Lady: In faith, for little England you would venture an emballing.

I myself would for Carnarvonshire, although there longed no more to the crown but that.

Lord, who comes here?

(Chamberlain enters)

Lord Chamberlain: Good morrow, ladies.

What were it worth to know, the secret of your conference?

Anne Bullen: My good lord, not your demand; it values not your asking.

Our mistress' sorrows we were pitying.

Lord Chamberlain: It was a gentle business, and becoming the action of good women: there is hope , all will be well.

Anne Bullen: Now, I pray God, amen!

Lord Chamberlain: You bear a gentle mind, and heavenly blessings follow such creatures.

That you may, fair lady, perceive I speak sincerely and high note's taken of your many virtues, the king's majesty commends his good opinion of you, and does purpose honour to you no less flowing than Marchioness of Pembroke; to which title a thousand pound a year, annual support, out of his grace he adds.

Anne Bullen: I do not know what kind of my obedience I should tender more than my all is nothing; nor my prayers are not words duly hallowed, nor my wishes more worth than empty vanities, yet prayers and wishes are all I can return.

Beseech your lordship, Vouchsafe to speak my thanks and my obedience, as from a blushing handmaid, to his highness; whose health and royalty I pray for.

Lord Chamberlain: Lady, I shall not fail to approve the fair conceit the king hath of you.

(From Aside)

I have perused her well, beauty and honour in her are so mingled that they have caught the king, and who knows yet but from this lady may proceed a gem to lighten all this isle?

I'll to the king, and say I spoke with you.

(Chamberlain exits)

Anne Bullen: My honoured lord.

Old Lady: Why, this it is; see, see!

I have been begging sixteen years in court, am yet a courtier beggarly, nor could come pat betwixt too early and too late, for any suit of pounds; and you oh fate!

A very fresh-fish here, fie, fie, fie upon this compelled fortune!, have your mouth filled up before you open it.

Anne Bullen: This is strange to me.

Old Lady: How tastes it? Is it bitter? Forty pence, no.

There was a lady once, it is an old story, that would not be a queen, that would she not; for all the mud in Egypt: have you heard it?

Anne Bullen: Come, you are pleasant.

Old Lady: With your theme, I could overmount the lark.

The Marchioness of Pembroke!

A thousand pounds a year for pure respect!

No other obligation! By my life, that promises more thousands; honour's train is longer than his foreskirt.

By this time I know your back will bear a duchess; say, are you not stronger than you were?

Anne Bullen: Good lady, make yourself mirth with your particular fancy and leave me out on it.

Would I had no being, if this salute my blood a jot, it faints me to think what follows the queen is comfortless, and we forgetful in our long absence: pray.

Do not deliver what here you've heard to her.

Old Lady: What do you think me?

(Exeunt)

Act II, Scene 4

A hall in Black-Friars.

(Trumpets, sonnet, and cornets)

Vergers with short silver wands enter, next them two Scribes in the habit of doctors,

(Canterbury enters)

(Lincoln, Ely, Rochester, and Saint Asaph enter)

(after some distance a gentleman bearing the purse, with the great seal and a cardinal's hat enters)

(Two Priests bearing each a silver cross, then a bare-headed Gentleman-usher accompanied with a Sergeant-at-arms bearing a silver mace enter)

(Two Gentlemen bearing two great silver pillars after them, side by side enter)

(Cardinal Wolsey and Cardinal Campeius; two Noblemen (p)with the sword and mace enter).

(King Henry VIII takes place under the cloth of state, Cardinal Wolsey and Cardinal Campeius sit under him as judges)

(Queen Katharine takes place some distance from King Henry VIII)

(The Bishops place themselves on each side the court, in manner of a consistory; below them, the Scribes)

(The Lords sit next the Bishops)

(The rest of the Attendants stand in convenient order about the stage)

Cardinal Wolsey: Whilst our commission from Rome is read, let silence be commanded.

Henry VIII: What's the need?

It hath already publicly been read, and on all sides the authority allowed; you may, then, spare that time.

Cardinal Wolsey: Be it so, proceed.

Scribe: Say, Henry King of England, come into the court.

Crier: Henry King of England, &c.

Henry VIII: Here.

Scribe: Say, Katharine Queen of England, come into the court.

Crier: Katharine Queen of England

(Queen Katharine makes no answer, rises out of her chair, goes about the court, comes to King Henry VIII, and kneels at his feet; then speaks)

Queen Katharine: Sir, I desire you do me right and justice; and to bestow your pity on me.

For I am a most poor woman, and a stranger born out of your dominions, having here no judge indifferent, nor no more assurance of equal friendship and proceeding.

Alas, sir, in what have I offended you?

What cause hath my behavior given to your displeasure that thus you should proceed to put me off, and take your good grace from me?

Heaven witness, I have been to you a true and humble wife, at all times to your will conformable; ever in fear to kindle your dislike, yea, subject to your countenance glad or sorry as I saw it inclined.

When was the hour I ever contradicted your desire, or made it not mine too? Or which of your friends have I not strove to love, although I knew he were mine enemy?

What friend of mine that had to him derived your anger, did I continue in my liking? Nay, gave notice, he was from thence discharged.

Sir, call to mind that I have been your wife, in this obedience, upward of twenty years and have been blest with many children by you.

If in the course and process of this time you can report and prove it too, against mine honour aught, my bond to wedlock, or my love and duty against your sacred person, in God's name turn me away and let the foul'st contempt shut door upon me.

So give me up to the sharp'st kind of justice if it please you sir, the king; your father was reputed for a prince most prudent, of an excellent and unmatched wit and judgment.

Ferdinand, my father, king of Spain, was reckoned one of the wisest prince that there had reigned by many a year before.

It is not to be questioned that they had gathered a wise council to them of every realm, that did debate this business; who deemed our marriage lawful.

Wherefore I humbly beseech you, sir, to spare me, till I may be by my friends in Spain advised; whose counsel I will implore: if not, in the name of God, your pleasure be fulfilled!

Cardinal Wolsey: You have here, lady, and of your choice, these reverend fathers; men of singular integrity and learning, yea, the elect of the land who are assembled to plead your cause.

It shall be therefore bootless that longer you desire the court; as well for your own quiet, as to rectify what is unsettled in the king.

Cardinal Campeius: His grace hath spoken well and justly, therefore, madam, it's fit this royal session do proceed; and that without delay their arguments be now produced and heard.

Queen Katharine: Lord cardinal, to you I speak.

Cardinal Wolsey: Your pleasure, madam?

Queen Katharine: Sir, I am about to weep, but thinking that we are a queen, or long have dreamed so, certain the daughter of a king, my drops of tears I'll turn to sparks of fire.

Cardinal Wolsey: Be patient yet.

Queen Katharine: I will, when you are humble; nay, before or God will punish me.

I do believe, induced by potent circumstances, that you are mine enemy and make my challenge, you shall not be my judge.

For it is you who have blown this coal between my lord and me, which God's dew quench! Therefore I say again I utterly abhor, yea, from my soul refuse you for my judge; whom yet once more I hold my most malicious foe, and think not at all a friend to truth.

Cardinal Wolsey: I do profess you speak not like yourself, whoever yet have stood to charity and displayed the effects of disposition gentle, and of wisdom overtopping woman's power.

Madam, you do me wrong, I have no spleen against you; nor injustice for you or any: how far I have proceeded, or how far further shall, is warranted by a commission from the consistory; yea the whole consistory of Rome.

You charge me that I have blown this coal, I do deny it.

The king is present, if it be known to him that I gainsay my deed, how may he wound, and worthily my falsehood! Yea, as much as you have done my truth, if he know that I am free of your report, he knows I am not of your wrong;

Therefore, in him it lies to cure me: and the cure is, to remove these thoughts from you: the which before his highness shall speak in; I do beseech you, gracious madam, to unthink your speaking and to say so no more.

Queen Katharine: My lord, my lord, I am a simple woman, much too weak to oppose your cunning.

You're meek and humble-mouthed, you sign your place and calling, in full seeming with meekness and humility; but your heart is crammed with arrogancy, spleen, and pride.

You have, by fortune and his highness' favours, gone slightly o'er low steps and now are mounted; where powers are your retainers, and your words domestics to you, serve your will, as it please yourself pronounce their office.

I must tell you, you tender more your person's honour than your high profession spiritual, that again I do refuse you for my judge; and here before you all, appeal unto the pope to bring my whole cause 'fore his holiness and to be judged by him.

(She curtsies to King Henry VIII, and offers to depart)

Cardinal Campeius: The queen is obstinate, stubborn to justice, apt to accuse it, and disdainful to be tried by it.

It is not well, she's going away.

Henry VIII: Call her again.

Crier: Katharine Queen of England, come into the court.

Griffith: Madam, you are called back.

Queen Katharine: What need you note it? Pray you, keep your way.

When you are called, return.

Now, the Lord help me, they vex me past my patience!

Pray you, pass on, I will not tarry; no, nor ever more upon this business my appearance make in any of their courts.

(Exeunt Queen Katharine and her Attendants)

Henry VIII: Go thy ways, Kate.

That man in the world who shall report he has a better wife, let him in nought be trusted for speaking false, in that thou art alone.

If thy rare qualities, sweet gentleness, thy meekness saint-like, wife-like government, obeying in commanding and thy parts sovereign and pious else could speak thee out the queen of earthly queens.

She's noble born and like her true nobility, she has carried herself towards me.

Cardinal Wolsey: Most gracious sir, in humblest manner I require your highness.

That it shall please you to declare, in hearing of all these ears for where I am robbed and bound, there must I be unloosed, although not there at once and fully satisfied, whether ever I did broach this business to your highness; or laid any scruple in your way, which might induce you to the question on it? Or ever?

Have to you, but with thanks to God for such a royal lady spoke one the least word that might be to the prejudice of her present state, or touch of her good person?

Henry VIII: My lord cardinal, I do excuse you; yea, upon mine honour, I free you from it.

You are not to be taught that you have many enemies that know not why they are so, but, like to village-curs bark when their fellows do.

By some of these the queen is put in anger.

You're excused, but will you be more justified?

You ever have wished the sleeping of this business, never desired it to be stirred but often have hindered, often, the passages made toward it.

On my honour, I speak my good lord cardinal to this point and thus far clear him.

Now, what moved me to it, I will be bold with time and your attention.

Then mark the inducement, thus it came; give heed to it.

My conscience first received a tenderness, scruple, and prick, on certain speeches uttered by the Bishop of Bayonne, then French ambassador; who had been hither sent on the debating a marriage between the Duke of Orleans and our daughter Mary.

In the progress of this business, were a determinate resolution, he, I mean the bishop did require a respite; wherein he might the king his lord advertise whether our daughter were legitimate, respecting this our marriage with the dowager, sometimes our brother's wife.

This respite shook the bosom of my conscience, entered me,

Yea, with a splitting power, and made to tremble the region of my breast, which forced such way that many amazed considerings did throng and pressed in with this caution.

First, methought I stood not in the smile of heaven, who had commanded nature that my lady's womb if it conceived a male child by me; should do no more offices of life to it than the grave does to the dead.

For her male issue, or died where they were made, or shortly after this world had aired them; hence I took a thought, this was a judgment on me, that my kingdom well worthy the best heir of the world should not be gladded in it by me.

Then follows, that I weighed the danger which my realms stood in by this my issue's fail; and that gave to me many a groaning throe.

Thus hulling in the wild sea of my conscience, I did steer toward this remedy whereupon we are now present here together: that's to say, I meant to rectify my conscience, which I then did feel full sick, and yet not well.

By all the reverend fathers of the land and doctors learned.

First I began in private with you, my Lord of Lincoln, you remember how under my oppression I did reek when I first moved you.

Bishop Lincoln: Very well, my liege.

Henry VIII: I have spoke long.

Be pleased yourself to say how far you satisfied me.

Bishop Lincoln: So please your highness, the question did at first so stagger me, bearing a state of mighty moment in it and consequence of dread that I committed the daring'st counsel which I had to doubt; and did entreat your highness to this course which you are running here.

Henry VIII: I then moved you, my Lord of Canterbury; and got your leave to make this present summons.

Unsolicited I left no reverend person in this court, but by particular consent proceeded under your hands and seal; therefore go on.

For no dislike in the world against the person of the good queen, but the sharp thorny points of my alleged reasons drive this forward.

Prove but our marriage lawful, by my life and kingly dignity, we are contented to wear our mortal state to come with her, Katharine our queen, before the primest creature that's paragoned on' the world.

Cardinal Campeius: So please your highness, the queen being absent; it is a needful fitness that we adjourn this court till further day.

Meanwhile, must be an earnest motion made to the queen, to call back her appeal she intends unto his holiness.

Henry VIII: **(From Aside)** I may perceive these cardinals trifle with me.

I abhor this dilatory sloth and tricks of Rome.

My learned and well-beloved servant, Cranmer, pray I to thee return with thy approach, I know my comfort comes along.

Break up the court.

I say, set on.

(Exeunt in manner as they entered)

Act III, Scene 1

Queen Katharine's apartments. (London)

(Queen Katharine and her Women enters as at work)

Queen Katharine: Take thy lute, wench.

My soul grows sad with troubles; sing, and disperse them if thou canst.

(Leaves working)

(Song)

Orpheus with his lute made trees, and the mountain tops that freeze; bow themselves when he did sing.

To his music plants and flowers, ever sprung; as sun and showers there had made a lasting spring.

Everything that heard him play, even the billows of the sea hung their heads, and then lay by.

In sweet music is such art, killing care and grief of heart fall asleep, or hearing, die.

(A Gentleman enters)

Queen Katharine: How now!

Gentleman: An't please your grace, the two great cardinals wait in the presence.

Queen Katharine: Would they speak with me?

Gentleman: They willed me say so, madam.

Queen Katharine: Pray their graces to come near.

(Gentleman exits)

What can be their business with me, a poor weak woman, fallen from favour?

I do not like their coming.

Now I think on it, they should be good men; their affairs as righteous, but all hoods make not monks.

(Cardinal Wolsey and Cardinal Campeius enter)

Cardinal Wolsey: Peace to your highness!

Queen Katharine: Your graces find me here part of a housewife, I would be all, against the worst may happen.

What are your pleasures with me, reverend lords?

Cardinal Wolsey: May it please you noble madam, to withdraw into your private chamber, we shall give you the full cause of our coming.

Queen Katharine: Speak it here, there's nothing I have done yet, of my conscience deserves a corner; would all other women, could all other woman speak this with as free a soul as I do!

My lords, I care not, so much I am happy above a number, if my actions were tried by every tongue, every eye saw them; envy and base opinion set against them, I know my life so even.

If your business seek me out, and that way I am wife in, out with it boldly.

Truth loves open dealing.

Cardinal Wolsey: Tanta est erga te mentis integritas, regina serenissima…

Queen Katharine: Oh good my lord, no Latin; I am not such a truant since my coming, as not to know the language I have lived in.

A strange tongue makes my cause more strange, suspicious; I pray you, speak in English.

Here are some will thank you, if you speak truth, for their poor mistress' sake; believe me, she has had much wrong.

Lord cardinal, The willing'st sin I ever yet committed may be absolved in English.

Cardinal Wolsey: Noble lady, I am sorry my integrity should breed and service to his majesty and you; so deep suspicion where all faith was meant.

We come not by the way of accusation to taint that honour every good tongue blesses, nor to betray you any way to sorrow; you have too much, good lady, but to know how you stand minded in the weighty difference between the king and you; and to deliver, like free and honest men our just opinions, and comforts to your cause.

Cardinal Campeius: Most honoured madam, my Lord of York, out of his noble nature,

Zeal and obedience he still bore your grace; forgetting like a good man, your late censure both of his truth and him, which was too far.

Offers, as I do, in a sign of peace, his service and his counsel.

Queen Katharine: (From Aside) To betray me.

My lords, I thank you both for your good wills; ye speak like honest men, pray God ye prove so!

How to make ye suddenly an answer? In such a point of weight, so near mine honour more near my life I fear, with my weak wit, and to such men of gravity and learning.

In truth, I know not.

I was set at work among my maids, full little, God knows, looking either for such men or such business.

For her sake that I have been, for I feel the last fit of my greatness; good, your graces let me have time and counsel for my cause.

Alas, I am a woman, friendless, hopeless!

Cardinal Wolsey: Madam, you wrong the king's love with these fears.

Your hopes and friends are infinite.

Queen Katharine: In England, but little for my profit can you think, lords, that any Englishman dare give me counsel?

Or be a known friend, against his highness pleasure, though he be grown so desperate to be honest, and live a subject?

Nay, forsooth, my friends, they that must weigh out my afflictions, they that my trust must grow to, live not here.

They are, as all my other comforts, far hence in mine own country, lords.

Cardinal Campeius: I would your grace would leave your griefs, and take my counsel.

Queen Katharine: How, sir?

Cardinal Campeius: Put your main cause into the king's protection, he's loving and most gracious.

It will be much both for your honour better and your cause, for if the trial of the law overtake ye, you'll part away disgraced.

Cardinal Wolsey: He tells you rightly.

Queen Katharine: Ye tell me what ye wish for both, my ruin; is this your Christian counsel?

Out upon ye!

Heaven is above all yet; there sits a judge that no king can corrupt.

Cardinal Campeius: Your rage mistakes us.

Queen Katharine: The more shame for ye holy men, I thought upon my soul ye two reverend cardinal were filled with virtues; but cardinal sins and hollow hearts I fear ye be.

Mend them, for shame, my lords.

Is this your comfort?

The cordial that ye bring a wretched lady, a woman lost among ye, laughed at, scorned?

I will not wish ye half my miseries, I have more charity; but say I warned ye.

Take heed, for heaven's sake, take heed, lest at once the burthen of my sorrows fall upon ye.

Cardinal Wolsey: Madam, this is a mere distraction, you turn the good we offer into envy

Queen Katharine: Ye turn me into nothing: woe upon ye

And all such false professors! Would you have me, if you have any justice, any pity; if ye be anything but churchmen's habits, put my sick cause into his hands that hates me?

Alas, has banished me his bed already, his love too long ago! I am old, my lords, and all the fellowship I hold now with him is only my obedience.

What can happen to me above this wretchedness?

All your studies make me a curse like this.

Cardinal Campeius: Your fears are worse.

Queen Katharine: Have I lived thus long, let me speak myself, since virtue finds no friends, a wife, a true one?

A woman, I dare say without vain-glory, never yet branded with suspicion?

Have I with all my full affections still met the king? Loved him next heaven?

Obeyed him? Been, out of fondness, superstitious to him?

Almost forgot my prayers to content him? And am I thus rewarded?

It is not well, lords.

Bring me a constant woman to her husband, one that never dreamed a joy beyond his pleasure; and to that woman when she has done most; yet will I add an honour, a great patience.

Cardinal Wolsey: Madam, you wander from the good we aim at.

Queen Katharine: My lord, I dare not make myself so guilty, to give up willingly that noble title your master wed me to; nothing but death shall ever divorce my dignities.

Cardinal Wolsey: Pray, hear me.

Queen Katharine: Would I had never trod this English earth, or felt the flatteries that grow upon it!

Ye have angels' faces, but heaven knows your hearts.

What will become of me now, wretched lady!

I am the most unhappy woman living.

Alas, poor wenches, where are now your fortunes!

Shipwrecked upon a kingdom, where no pity, no friend, no hope; no kindred weep for me; almost no grave allowed me.

Like the lily that once was mistress of the field and flourished, I'll hang my head and perish.

Cardinal Wolsey: If your grace could but be brought to know our ends are honest, you would feel more comfort.

Why should we, good lady, upon what cause wrong you?

Alas, our places, the way of our profession is against it.

We are to cure such sorrows, not to sow them.

For goodness' sake, consider what you do; how you may hurt yourself, ay, utterly grow from the king's acquaintance, by this carriage.

The hearts of princes kiss obedience, so much they love it, but to stubborn spirits they swell and grow as terrible as storms.

I know you have a gentle, noble temper, a soul as even as a calm.

Pray, think us those we profess, peace-makers, friends, and servants.

Cardinal Campeius: Madam, you'll find it so.

You wrong your virtues with these weak women's fears; a noble spirit as yours was put into you, ever casts such doubts, as false coin, from it.

The king loves you, beware you lose it not.

For us, if you please, to trust us in your business, we are ready to use our utmost studies in your service.

Queen Katharine: Do what ye will, my lords.

And, pray, forgive me, if I have used myself unmannerly; you know I am a woman, lacking wit to make a seemly answer to such persons.

Pray, do my service to his majesty.

He has my heart yet; and shall have my prayers while I shall have my life.

Come, reverend fathers, bestow your counsels on me.

She now begs that little thought, when she set footing here, she should have bought her dignities so dear.

(Exeunt)

Act III, Scene 2

Ante-chamber to King Henry VIII's apartment.

(Norfolk, Suffolk, Surrey, and Chamberlain enter)

Duke of Norfolk: If you will now unite in your complaints and force them with a constancy; the cardinal cannot stand under them: if you omit the offer of this time, I cannot promise but that you shall sustain more new disgraces with these you bear already.

Earl of Surrey: I am joyful to meet the least occasion that may give me remembrance of my father-in-law, the duke, to be revenged on him.

Duke of Suffolk: Which of the peers have uncontemned gone by him, or at least strangely neglected?

When did he regard the stamp of nobleness in any person out of himself?

Lord Chamberlain: My lords, you speak your pleasures.

What he deserves of you and me I know, what we can do to him, though now the time gives way to us, I much fear.

If you cannot bar his access to the king, never attempt anything on him; for he hath a witchcraft over the king in's tongue.

Duke of Norfolk: Oh fear him not; his spell in that is out.

The king hath found matter against him that for ever mars the honey of his language.

No, he's settled; not to come off, in his displeasure.

Earl of Surrey: Sir, I should be glad to hear such news as this once every hour.

Duke of Norfolk: Believe it, this is true.

In the divorce his contrary proceedings are all unfolded wherein he appears as I would wish mine enemy.

Earl of Surrey: How came his practises to light?

Duke of Suffolk: Most strangely.

Earl of Surrey: Oh how, how?

Duke of Suffolk: The cardinal's letters to the pope miscarried, and came to the eye of the king; wherein was read, how that the cardinal did entreat his holiness to stay the judgment of the divorce; for if it did take place, I do, quoth he, perceive my king is tangled in affection to a creature of the queen's.

Lady Anne Bullen.

Earl of Surrey: Has the king this?

Duke of Suffolk: Believe it.

Earl of Surrey: Will this work?

Lord Chamberlain: The king in this perceives him, how he coasts and hedges his own way; but in this point all his tricks founder, and he brings his physic after his patient's death.

The king already hath married the fair lady.

Earl of Surrey: Would he had!

Duke of Suffolk: May you be happy in your wish, my lord

For, I profess, you have it.

Earl of Surrey: Now, all my joy

Trace the conjunction!

Duke of Suffolk: My amen to it!

Duke of Norfolk: All men's!

Duke of Suffolk: There's order given for her coronation:

Marry, this is yet but young, and may be left

To some ears unrecounted. But, my lords, 1890

She is a gallant creature, and complete

In mind and feature: I persuade me, from her

Will fall some blessing to this land, which shall in it be memorised.

Earl of Surrey: But, will the king digest this letter of the cardinal's?

The Lord forbid!

Duke of Norfolk: Marry, amen!

Duke of Suffolk: No, no, there be more wasps that buzz about his nose will make this sting the sooner.

Cardinal Campeius is stolen away to Rome, hath taken no leave, has left the cause on the king unhandled; and is posted as the agent of our cardinal, to second all his plot.

I do assure you the king cried: Ha! at this.

Lord Chamberlain: Now, God incense him, and let him cry Ha! louder!

Duke of Norfolk: But, my lord,

When returns Cranmer?

Duke of Suffolk: He is returned in his opinions; which have satisfied the king for his divorce; together with all famous colleges almost in Christendom.

Shortly, I believe, his second marriage shall be published, and her coronation.

Katharine no more shall be called queen, but princess dowager and widow to Prince Arthur.

Duke of Norfolk: This same Cranmer's a worthy fellow, and hath taken much pain in the king's business.

Duke of Suffolk: He has; and we shall see him for it an archbishop.

Duke of Norfolk: So I hear.

Duke of Suffolk: It is so.

The cardinal!

(Cardinal Wolsey and Cromwell enter)

Duke of Norfolk: Observe, observe, he's moody.

Cardinal Wolsey: The packet.

Cromwell: Gave it you the king?

Cromwell: To his own hand, in's bedchamber.

Cardinal Wolsey: Looked he on the inside of the paper?

Cromwell: Presently he did unseal them, and the first he viewed, he did it with a serious mind; a heed was in his countenance.

You he bade attend him here this morning.

Cardinal Wolsey: Is he ready to come abroad?

Cromwell: I think, by this he is.

Cardinal Wolsey: Leave me awhile.

(Cromwell exits)

(From Aside)

It shall be to the Duchess of Alencon, the French king's sister: he shall marry her.

Anne Bullen! No; I'll no Anne Bullens for him.

There's more in it than fair visage. Bullen!

No, we'll have no Bullens.

Speedily, I wish to hear from Rome.

The Marchioness of Pembroke!

Duke of Norfolk: He's discontented.

Duke of Suffolk: May be, he hears the king does whet his anger to him.

Earl of Surrey: Sharp enough, Lord, for thy justice!

Cardinal Wolsey: (From Aside) The late queen's gentlewoman, a knight's daughter to be her mistress' mistress!

The queen's queen!

This candle burns not clear, it is… I must snuff it.

Then out it goes.

What though I know her virtuous and well deserving?

Yet I know her for a spleeny Lutheran; and not wholesome to our cause, that she should lie in the bosom of our hard-ruled king.

Again, there is sprung up an heretic, an arch one, cranmer; one Hath crawled into the favour of the king and is his oracle.

Duke of Norfolk: He is vexed at something.

Earl of Surrey: I would it were something that would fret the string, the master-cord on his heart!

(King Henry VIII enters reading of a schedule, with Lovell)

Duke of Suffolk: The king, the king!

Henry VIII: What piles of wealth hath he accumulated to his own portion! And what expense by the hour seems to flow from him!

How, in the name of thrift, does he rake this together! Now, my lords, saw you the cardinal?

Duke of Norfolk: My lord, we have stood here observing him, some strange commotion is in his brain.

He bites his lip and starts, stops on a sudden, looks upon the ground then lays his finger on his temple; straight springs out into fast gait, then stops again, strikes his breast hard and anon he casts his eye against the moon.

In most strange postures we have seen him set himself.

Henry VIII: It may well be, there is a mutiny in's mind.

This morning papers of state he sent me to peruse, as I required; and wanting you, what I found there, on my conscience was put unwittingly?

Forsooth, an inventory, thus importing; the several parcels of his plate, his treasure, rich stuffs, and ornaments of household; which I find at such proud rate, that it out-speaks possession of a subject.

Duke of Norfolk: It's heaven's will.

Some spirit put this paper in the packet to bless your eye withal.

Henry VIII: If we did think his contemplation were above the earth and fixed on spiritual object, he should still dwell in his musings; but I am afraid his thinkings are below the moon, not worth his serious considering.

(King Henry VIII takes his seat; whispers Lovell who goes to Cardinal Wolsey)

Cardinal Wolsey: Heaven forgive me!

Ever God bless your highness!

Henry VIII: Good my lord, you are full of heavenly stuff, and bear the inventory of your best graces in your mind; the which you were now running over.

You have scarce time to steal from spiritual leisure a brief span, to keep your earthly audit.

Sure, in that I deem you an ill husband, and am glad to have you therein my companion.

Cardinal Wolsey: Sir, for holy offices I have a time; a time to think upon the part of business which I bear in the state; and nature does require her times of preservation, which perforce I, her frail son amongst my brethren mortal must give my tendence to.

Henry VIII: You have said well.

Cardinal Wolsey: And ever may your highness yoke together, as I will lend you cause, my doing well with my well saying!

Henry VIII: It is well said again, and it is a kind of good deed to say well; and yet words are no deeds.

My father loved you.

His said he did; and with his deed did crown his word upon you, since I had my office; I have kept you next my heart, have not alone employed you where high profits might come home, but pared my present savings to bestow my bounties upon you.

Cardinal Wolsey: **(From Aside)** What should this mean?

Earl of Surrey: **(From Aside)** The Lord increase this business!

Henry VIII: Have I not made you, the prime man of the state?

I pray you, tell me if what I now pronounce you have found true.

And if you may confess it, say withal if you are bound to us or no.

What say you?

Cardinal Wolsey: My sovereign, I confess your royal graces showered on me daily, have been more than could my studied purposes requite; which went beyond all man's endeavours.

My endeavours have ever come too short of my desires, yet filed with my abilities: mine own ends have been mine so that evermore they pointed to the good of your most sacred person and the profit of the state.

For your great graces heaped upon me, poor undeserver, I can nothing render but allegiant thanks, my prayers to heaven for you, my loyalty; whichever has and ever shall be growing till death, that winter kill it.

Henry VIII: Fairly answered, a loyal and obedient subject is therein illustrated.

The honour of it does pay the act of it, as in the contrary the foulness is the punishment.

I presume that as my hand has opened bounty to you, my heart dropped love, my power rained honour, more on you than any; so your hand and heart your brain, and every function of your power should; notwithstanding that your bond of duty, as it were in love's particular, be more To me, your friend, than any.

Cardinal Wolsey: I do profess that for your highness' good I ever laboured more than mine own; that am, have, and will be, though all the world should crack their duty to you and throw it from their soul.

Though perils did abound, as thick as thought could make them, and appear in forms more horrid, yet my duty as doth a rock against the chiding flood, should the approach of this wild river break, and stand unshaken yours.

Henry VIII: It is nobly spoken.

Take notice, lords, he has a loyal breast, for you have seen him open it.

Read over this.

(Giving him papers)

And after, this: and then to breakfast with what appetite you have.

(King Henry VIII exits frowning upon Cardinal Wolsey, the Nobles throng after him, smiling and whispering)

Cardinal Wolsey: What should this mean?

What sudden anger's this? How have I reaped it?

He parted frowning from me as if ruin, leaped from his eyes.

So looks the chafed lion upon the daring huntsman that has galled him, then makes him nothing.

I must read this paper; I fear, the story of his anger.

It is so, this paper has undone me.

It is the account of all that world of wealth I have drawn together for mine own ends; indeed, to gain the popedom and fee my friends in Rome.

Oh negligence! Fit for a fool to fall by: what cross devil made me put this main secret in the packet I sent the king? Is there no way to cure this?

No new device to beat this from his brains?

I know it will stir him strongly, yet I know a way if it take right that speaks in spite of fortune and will bring me off again.

What's this? To the Pope!

The letter, as I live, with all the business I write to his holiness.

Nay then, farewell!

I have touched the highest point of all my greatness; and from that full meridian of my glory, I haste now to my setting.

I shall fall like a bright exhalation m the evening, and no man see me more.

(Re-enter to Cardinal Wolsey, Norfolk and Suffolk, Surrey and the Chamberlain)

Duke of Norfolk: Hear the king's pleasure, cardinal: who commands you to render up the great seal presently into our hands; and to confine yourself to Asher House, my Lord of Winchester's, till you hear further from his highness.

Cardinal Wolsey: Stay.

Where's your commission, lords? Words cannot carry authority so weighty.

Duke of Suffolk: Who dare cross them bearing the king's will from his mouth expressly?

Cardinal Wolsey: Till I find more than will or words to do it, I mean your malice know, officious lords, I dare and must deny it.

Now I feel of what coarse metal ye are moulded, envy.

How eagerly ye follow my disgraces, as if it fed ye! And how sleek and wanton ye appear in everything may bring my ruin!

Follow your envious courses, men of malice; you have Christian warrant for them, and no doubt in time will find their fit rewards.

That seal, you ask with such a violence, the king, mine and your master with his own hand gave me, bade me enjoy it with the place and honours during my life; and to confirm his goodness; tied it by letters-patents: now, who'll take it?

Earl of Surrey: The king, that gave it.

Cardinal Wolsey: It must be himself, then.

Earl of Surrey: Thou art a proud traitor, priest.

Cardinal Wolsey: Proud lord, thou liest within these forty hours Surrey durst better have burnt that tongue than said so.

Earl of Surrey: Thy ambition, thou scarlet sin, robbed this bewailing land of noble Buckingham, my father-in-law.

The heads of all thy brother cardinals, with thee and all thy best parts bound together, weighed not a hair of his.

Plague of your policy! You sent me deputy for Ireland, far from his succor, from the king, from all that might have mercy on the fault thou gavest him; whilst your great goodness, out of holy pity absolved him with an axe.

Cardinal Wolsey: This, and all else this talking lord can lay upon my credit, I answer is most false.

The duke, by law, found his deserts.

How innocent I was from any private malice in his end, his noble jury and foul cause can witness.

If I loved many words, lord, I should tell you, you have as little honesty as honour that in the way of loyalty and truth toward the king, my ever royal master, dare mate a sounder man than Surrey can be, and all that love his follies.

Earl of Surrey: By my soul, your long priest coat protects you, thou shouldst feel my sword in the life-blood of thee else.

My lords, Can ye endure to hear this arrogance? And from this fellow? If we live thus tamely, to be thus jaded by a piece of scarlet.

Farewell nobility, let his grace go forward and dare us with his cap like larks.

Cardinal Wolsey: All goodness is poison to thy stomach.

Earl of Surrey: Yes, that goodness of gleaning all the land's wealth into one into your own hands, cardinal, by extortion.

The goodness of your intercepted packets, you write to the pope against the king, your goodness, since you provoke me, shall be most notorious.

My Lord of Norfolk, as you are truly noble, as you respect the common good; the state of our despised nobility, our issues, who if he live will scarce be gentlemen; produce the grand sum of his sins, the articles collected from his life.

I'll startle you worse than the scaring bell, when the brown wench lay kissing in your arms, lord cardinal.

Cardinal Wolsey: How much, methinks, I could despise this man, but that I am bound in charity against it!

Duke of Norfolk: Those articles, my lord, are in the king's hand, but thus much, they are foul ones.

Cardinal Wolsey: So much fairer and spotless shall mine innocence arise when the king knows my truth.

Earl of Surrey: This cannot save you.

I thank my memory, I yet remember some of these articles; and out they shall now, if you can blush and cry: guilty, cardinal, you'll show a little honesty.

Cardinal Wolsey: Speak on, sir, I dare your worst objections.

If I blush, it is to see a nobleman want manners.

Earl of Surrey: I had rather want those than my head.

Have at you!

First, that, without the king's assent or knowledge, you wrought to be a legate, by which power you maimed the jurisdiction of all bishops.

Duke of Norfolk: Then, that in all you writ to Rome, or else to foreign princes, ego and Rex muse was still inscribed; in which you brought the king to be your servant.

Duke of Suffolk: Then that, without the knowledge either of king or council, when you went Ambassador to the emperor, you made bold to carry into Flanders the great seal.

Earl of Surrey: Item, you sent a large commission to Gregory de Cassado, to conclude, without the king's will or the state's allowance, a league between his highness and Ferrara.

Duke of Suffolk: That, out of mere ambition, you have caused your holy hat to be stamped on the king's coin.

Earl of Surrey: Then that you have sent innumerable substance, by what means got, I leave to your own conscience to furnish Rome, and to prepare the ways you have for dignities; to the mere undoing of all the kingdom.

Many more there are, which, since they are of you, and odious I will not taint my mouth with.

Lord Chamberlain: Oh my lord, press not a falling man too far! I is virtue.

His faults lie open to the laws; let them, not you, correct him.

My heart weeps to see him so little of his great self.

Earl of Surrey: I forgive him.

Duke of Suffolk: Lord cardinal, the king's further pleasure is, because all those things you have done of late; by your power legatine within this kingdom, fall into the compass of a forewarning that therefore such a writ be sued against you; to forfeit all your goods, lands, tenements, Chattels, and whatsoever, and to be out of the king's protection.

This is my charge.

Duke of Norfolk: And so we'll leave you to your meditations how to live better.

For your stubborn answer about the giving back the great seal to us, the king shall know it, and, no doubt, shall thank you.

So fare you well, my little good lord cardinal.

(Exeunt all but Cardinal Wolsey)

Cardinal Wolsey: So farewell to the little good you bear me.

Farewell!

Along farewell, to all my greatness!

This is the state of man: to-day he puts forth the tender leaves of hopes; to-morrow blossoms and bears his blushing honours thick upon him.

The third day comes a frost, a killing frost, and when he thinks, good easy man; for surely his greatness is a-ripening that nips his root, and then he falls, as I do.

I have ventured like little wanton boys that swim on bladders, this many summers in a sea of glory, but far beyond my depth.

My high-blown pride at length broke under me and now has left me, weary and old with service, to the mercy of a rude stream that must for ever hide me.

Vain pomp and glory of this world, I hate ye.

I feel my heart new opened, oh how wretched is that poor man that hangs on princes' favours!

There is, betwixt that smile we would aspire to, that sweet aspect of princes, and their ruin, more pangs and fears than wars or women have.

And when he falls, he falls like Lucifer, never to hope again.

(Cromwell enters and stands amazed)

Why, how now, Cromwell!

Cromwell: I have no power to speak, sir.

Cardinal Wolsey: What, amazed at my misfortunes? Can thy spirit wonder

a great man should decline?

Nay, and you weep, I am fallen indeed.

Cromwell: How does your grace?

Cardinal Wolsey: Why, well; never so truly happy, my good.

Cromwell: I know myself now, and I feel within me a peace above all earthly dignities, a still and quiet conscience.

The king has cured me, I humbly thank his grace; and from these shoulders, these ruined pillars, out of pity; taken a load would sink a navy, too much honour.

Oh it is a burthen, Cromwell, it is a burthen too heavy for a man that hopes for heaven!

Cromwell: I am glad your grace has made that right use of it.

Cardinal Wolsey: I hope I have: I am able now, methinks, out of a fortitude of soul I feel;

to endure more miseries and greater far than my weak-hearted enemies dare offer.

What news abroad?

Cromwell: The heaviest and the worst is your displeasure with the king.

Cardinal Wolsey: God bless him!

Cromwell: The next is, that Sir Thomas More is chosen Lord chancellor in your place.

Cardinal Wolsey: That's somewhat sudden, but he's a learned man.

May he continue long in his highness' favour, and do justice for truth's sake and his conscience; that his bones when he has run his course and sleeps in blessings may have a tomb of orphans' tears wept on them!

What more?

Cromwell: That Cranmer is returned with welcome, installed lord archbishop of Canterbury.

Cardinal Wolsey: That's news indeed.

Cromwell: Last, that the Lady Anne, whom the king hath in secrecy long married; this day was viewed in open as his queen, going to chapel and the voice is now only about her coronation.

Cardinal Wolsey: There was the weight that pulled me down.

Oh Cromwell, the king has gone beyond me: all my glories in that one woman I have lost for ever.

No sun shall ever usher forth mine honours, or gild again the noble troops that waited upon my smiles.

Go, get thee from me, Cromwell; I am a poor fallen man unworthy now to be thy lord and master.

Seek the king, that sun I pray may never set! I have told him what and how true thou art.

He will advance thee; some little memory of me will stir him, I know his noble nature, not to let thy hopeful service perish too.

Good Cromwell, neglect him not, make use now and provide for thine own future safety.

Cromwell: Oh my lord, must I then leave you?

Must I needs forego so good, so noble and so true a master?

Bear witness, all that have not hearts of iron, with what a sorrow Cromwell leaves his lord.

The king shall have my service, but my prayers for ever and for ever shall be yours.

Cardinal Wolsey: Cromwell, I did not think to shed a tear in all my miseries, but thou hast forced me; out of thy honest truth to play the woman.

Let's dry our eyes: and thus far hear me, Cromwell; and when I am forgotten as I shall be, and sleep in dull cold marble, where no mention of me more must be heard of, say I, taught thee.

Say, Wolsey, that once trod the ways of glory, and sounded all the depths and shoals of honour, found thee a way out of his wreck, to rise in a sure and safe one; though thy master missed it.

Mark but my fall and that that ruined me.

Cromwell, I charge thee, fling away ambition.

By that sin fell the angels, how can man, then, the image of his Maker hope to win by it?

Love thyself last: cherish those hearts that hate thee, corruption wins not more than honesty.

Still in thy right hand carry gentle peace, to silence envious tongues.

Be just, and fear not.

Let all the ends thou aim'st at be thy country's, thy God's, and truth's; then if thou fall'st, oh Cromwell, thou fall'st a blessed martyr!

Serve the king and, pray to thee, lead me in.

There take an inventory of all I have, to the last penny; it is the king's: my robe and my integrity to heaven, is all I dare now call mine own.

Oh Cromwell, Cromwell!

Had I but served my God with half the zeal I served my king, he would not in mine age have left me naked to mine enemies.

Cromwell: Good sir, have patience.

Cardinal Wolsey: So I have. Farewell

The hopes of court! my hopes in heaven do dwell.

(Exeunt)

Act IV, Scene 1

A street in Westminster.

(Two Gentlemen enter, meeting one another)

First Gentleman: You're well met once again.

Second Gentleman: So are you.

First Gentleman: You come to take your stand here, and behold the Lady Anne pass from her coronation?

Second Gentleman: It is all my business.

At our last encounter, the Duke of Buckingham came from his trial.

First Gentleman: It is very true: but that time offered sorrow; this general joy.

Second Gentleman: It is well.

The citizens, I am sure, have shown at full their royal minds, as let them have their rights, they are ever forward; in celebration of this day with shows, Pageants and sights of honour.

First Gentleman: Never greater, nor, I'll assure you, better taken, sir.

Second Gentleman: May I be bold to ask at what that contains, that paper in your hand?

First Gentleman: Yes; 'tis the list of those that claim their offices this day by custom of the coronation.

The Duke of Suffolk is the first, and claims to be high-steward, next the Duke of Norfolk; he to be earl marshal.

You may read the rest.

Second Gentleman: I thank you, sir: had I not known those customs, I should have been beholding to your paper, but I beseech you, what's become of Katharine, the princess dowager?

How goes her business?

First Gentleman: That I can tell you too.

The Archbishop of Canterbury, accompanied with other learned and reverend fathers of his order, held a late court at Dunstable six miles off from Ampthill, where the princess lay; to which she was often cited by them, but appeared not.

And, to be short, for not appearance and the king's late scruple, by the main assent of all these learned men she was divorced; and the late marriage made of none effect since which she was removed to Kimbolton, where she remains now sick.

Second Gentleman: Alas, good lady!

(The trumpets sound)

(Announcement: stand close, the queen is coming)

(The order of the Coronation)

1: A lively flourish of Trumpets.

2: Then, two Judges.

3: Lord Chancellor, with the purse and mace before him.

4: Choristers, singing.

(Music)

5: Mayor of London, bearing the mace. Then Garter, in his coat of arms, and on his head a gilt copper crown.

6. Marquess Dorset, bearing a sceptre of gold, on his head a demi-coronal of gold. With him, Surrey, bearing the rod of silver with the dove, crowned with an earl's coronet.

7. Suffolk, in his robe of estate, his coronet is on his head bearing a long white wand, as high-steward. With him, Norfolk is with the rod of marshalship, a coronet on his head.

8. A canopy borne by four of the Cinque-ports; under it the Queen Anne in her robe; in her hair is a richly adorned crown with pearl.

On each side her, the Bishops of London and Winchester.

9. The old Duchess of Norfolk, in a coronal of gold, wrought with flowers, bearing Queen Anne's entourage.

10. Certain Ladies or Countesses, with plain circlets of gold without flowers.

(They pass over the stage in order and state)

Second Gentleman: A royal train, believe me.

These I know, who's that that bears the sceptre?

First Gentleman: Marquess Dorset, and that the Earl of Surrey, with the rod.

Second Gentleman: A bold brave gentleman that should be the Duke of Suffolk?

First Gentleman: 'Tis the same: high-steward.

Second **Gentleman:** And that my Lord of Norfolk?

First Gentleman: Yes.

Second Gentleman: Heaven bless thee!

(Looking on Queen Anne)

Thou hast the sweetest face I ever looked on.

Sir, as I have a soul, she is an angel, our king has all the Indies in his arms, and more and richer, when he strains that lady.

I cannot blame his conscience.

First Gentleman: They that bear the cloth of honour over her, are four barons of the Cinque-ports.

Second Gentleman: Those men are happy; and so are all are near her.

I take it, she that carries up the train is that old noble lady, Duchess of Norfolk.

First Gentleman: It is; and all the rest are countesses.

Second Gentleman: Their coronets say so. These are stars indeed, and sometimes falling ones.

First Gentleman: No more of that.

(Exit procession, and then a great flourish of trumpets)

(A third Gentleman enters)

First Gentleman: God save you, sir! Where have you been broiling?

Third Gentleman: Among the crowd in the Abbey where a finger could not be wedged in more.

I am stifled with the mere rankness of their joy.

Second Gentleman: You saw the ceremony?

Third Gentleman: That I did.

First Gentleman: How was it?

Third Gentleman: Well worth the seeing.

Second Gentleman: Good sir, speak it to us.

Third Gentleman: As well as I am able.

The rich stream of lords and ladies, having brought the queen to a prepared place in the choir fell off a distance from her; while her grace sat down to rest awhile, some half an hour or so in a rich chair of state, opposing freely the beauty of her person to the people.

Believe me, sir, she is the goodliest woman that ever lay by man, which when the people had the full view of, such a noise arose as the shrouds make at sea in a stiff tempest as loud; and to as many tunes.

Hats, cloaks, doublets, I think, flew up; and had their faces been loose, this day they had been lost.

Such joy I never saw before.

Great-bellied women, that had not half a week to go, like rams in the old time of war, would shake the press, and make them reel before them.

No man living could say if this is my wife' there; all were woven so strangely in one piece.

Second Gentleman: But, what followed?

Third Gentleman: At length her grace rose, and with modest paces came to the altar where she kneeled, and saint-like cast her fair eyes to heaven and prayed devoutly.

Then rose again and bowed her to the people.

When by the Archbishop of Canterbury she had all the royal makings of a queen as holy oil, Edward Confessor's crown, the rod, and bird of peace, and all such emblems laid nobly on her; which performed the choir with all the choicest music of the kingdom, together sung: A song of the Church.

So she parted, and with the same full state paced back again to York-place, where the feast is held.

First Gentleman: Sir, you must no more call it York-place, that's past; for, since the cardinal fell, that title's lost.

It is now the king's, and called Whitehall.

Third Gentleman: I know it, but it is so lately altered, that the old name is fresh about me.

Second Gentleman: What two reverend bishops were those that went on each side of the queen?

Third Gentleman: Stokesly and Gardiner; the one of Winchester, newly preferred from the king's secretary, the other, London.

Second Gentleman: He of Winchester Is held no great good lover of the archbishop's, the virtuous Cranmer.

Third Gentleman: All the land knows that.

However, yet there is no great breach; when it comes, cranmer will find a friend will not shrink from him.

Second Gentleman: Who may that be, I pray you?

Third Gentleman: Thomas Cromwell, a man in much esteem with the king, and truly a worthy friend.

The king has made him master of the jewel house, and one already of the privy council.

Second Gentleman: He will deserve more.

Third Gentleman: Yes, without all doubt.

Come, gentlemen, ye shall go my way, which is to the court, and there ye shall be my guests.

Something I can command, as I walk thither I'll tell ye more.

Both: You may command us, sir.

(Exeunt)

Act IV, Scene 2

Kimbolton.

(Katharine enters sick, led between Griffith, her gentleman usher, and Patience, her woman)

Griffith: How does your grace?

Queen Katharine: Oh Griffith, sick to death!

My legs, like loaden branches, bow to the earth, willing to leave their burthen.

Reach a chair, so now methinks I feel a little ease.

Didst thou not tell me, Griffith, as thou led'st me, that the great child of honour, Cardinal Wolsey, Was dead?

Griffith: Yes, madam; but I think your grace out of the pain you suffered, gave no ear to it.

Queen Katharine: Pray to thee, good Griffith, tell me how he died.

If well, he stepp'd before me, happily

For my example.

Griffith: Well, the voice goes, madam.

For after the stout Earl Northumberland arrested him at York, and brought him forward, as a man sorely tainted, to his answer; he fell sick suddenly, and grew so ill He could not sit his mule.

Queen Katharine: Alas, poor man!

Griffith: At last, with easy roads, he came to Leicester, lodged in the abbey; where the reverend abbot with all his covent, honourably received him; to whom he gave these words, oh father abbot, an old man, broken with the storms of state is come to lay his weary bones among ye; give him a little earth for charity!

So went to bed; where eagerly his sickness pursued him still: and, three nights after this, about the hour of eight, which he himself foretold should be his last, full of repentance, continual meditations, tears, and sorrows; he gave his honours to the world again his blessed part to heaven, and slept in peace.

Queen Katharine: So may he rest; his faults lie gently on him!

Yet thus far, Griffith, give me leave to speak him, and yet with charity.

He was a man of an unbounded stomach, ever ranking himself with princes; one that, by suggestions tied all the kingdom.

Simony was fair-play, his own opinion was his law; in the presence he would say untruths and be ever double both in his words and meaning.

He was never, but where he meant to ruin, pitiful.

His promises were as mighty as he then was, but his performance as he is now, nothing: of his own body he was ill, and gave the clergy in example.

Griffith: Noble madam, Men's evil manners live in brass; their virtues we write in water.

May it please your highness to hear me speak his good now?

Queen Katharine: Yes, good Griffith, I were malicious else.

Griffith: This cardinal, though from and humble stock undoubtedly, was fashioned to much honour from his cradle.

He was a scholar, and a ripe and good one, exceeding wise, fair-spoken, and persuading.

Lofty and sour to them that loved him not, but to those men that sought him sweet as summer, and though he were unsatisfied in getting which was a sin, yet in bestowing, madam he was most princely.

Ever witness for him those twins of learning that he raised in you, Ipswich and Oxford! One of which fell with him, unwilling to outlive the good that did it the other, though unfinished, yet so famous, so excellent in art and still so rising, that Christendom shall ever speak his virtue.

His overthrow heaped happiness upon him, for then, and not till then, he felt himself, and found the blessedness of being little.

And, to add greater honours to his age than man could give him, he died fearing God.

Queen Katharine: After my death I wish no other herald, no other speaker of my living actions to keep mine honour from corruption, but such an honest chronicler as Griffith.

Whom I most hated living, thou hast made me, with thy religious truth and modesty,

Now in his ashes honour, peace be with him!

Patience, be near me still and set me lower; I have not long to trouble thee.

Good Griffith, cause the musicians play me that sad note, I named my knell, whilst I sit meditating on that celestial harmony I go to.

(Sad and solemn music)

Griffith: She is asleep: good wench, let's sit down quiet for fear we wake her.

Softly, gentle Patience.

(Solemnly tripping one after another, six personages enter, clad in white robes wearing on their heads garlands of bays, and golden wizards on their faces; branches of bays or palm in their hands)

(They first congee unto her, then dance; and at certain changes, the first two hold a spare garland over her head; at which the other four make reverent curtsies; then the two that held the garland deliver the same to the other next two, who observe the

same order in their changes, and holding the garland over her head)

(Which done, they deliver the same garland to the last two, who likewise observe the same order at which, as it were by inspiration)

(She makes in her sleep signs of rejoicing, and holdeth up her hands to heaven in their dancing vanish, carrying the garland with them)

(The music continues)

Queen Katharine: Spirits of peace, where are ye? Are ye all gone, and leave me here in wretchedness behind ye?

Griffith: Madam, we are here.

Queen Katharine: It is not you I call for.

Saw ye none enter since I slept?

Griffith: None, madam.

Queen Katharine: No? Saw you not, even now, a blessed troop invite me to a banquet; whose bright faces cast thousand beams upon me, like the sun?

They promised me eternal happiness, and brought me garlands, Griffith, which I feel I am not worthy yet to wear.

I shall, assuredly.

Griffith: I am most joyful, madam, such good dreams possess your fancy.

Queen Katharine: Bid the music leave,

They are harsh and heavy to me.

(Music ceases)

Patience: Do you note

How much her grace is altered on the sudden?

How long her face is drawn? How pale she looks, and of an earthy cold? Mark her eyes!

Griffith: She is going, wench; pray, pray.

Patience: Heaven comfort her!

(A Messenger enters)

Messenger: And it please your grace…

Queen Katharine: You are a saucy fellow.

Deserve we no more reverence?

Griffith: You are to blame, knowing she will not lose her wonted greatness to use so rude behavior; go to kneel.

Messenger: I humbly do entreat your highness' pardon; my haste made me unmannerly.

There is staying a gentleman, sent from the king, to see you.

Queen Katharine: Admit him entrance, Griffith; but this fellow let me never see again.

(Exeunt Griffith and Messenger)

(Griffith re-enters with Capucius)

If my sight fail not, you should be lord ambassador from the emperor, my royal nephew, and your name Capucius.

Capucius: Madam, the same; your servant.

Queen Katharine: Oh, my lord, the times and titles now are altered strangely with me since first you knew me; but, I pray you, what is your pleasure with me?

Capucius: Noble lady, first mine own service to your grace; the next, the king's request that I would visit you, who grieves much for your weakness, and by me sends you his princely commendations, and heartily entreats you take good comfort.

Queen Katharine: Oh my good lord, that comfort comes too late; it is like a pardon after execution.

That gentle physic, given in time, had cured me, but now I am past an comforts here, but prayers.

How does his highness?

Capucius: Madam, in good health.

Queen Katharine: So may he ever do! And ever flourish when I shall dwell with worms, and my poor name banished the kingdom Patience, is that letter I caused you write, yet sent away?

Patience: No, madam.

(Giving it to Katharine)

Queen Katharine: Sir, I most humbly pray you to deliver this to my lord the king.

Capucius: Most willing, madam.

Queen Katharine: In which I have commended to his goodness the model of our chaste loves, his young daughter; the dews of heaven fall thick in blessings on her!

Beseeching him to give her virtuous breeding, she is young and of a noble modest nature, I hope she will deserve well; and a little to love her for her mother's sake, that loved him, Heaven knows how dearly.

My next poor petition is, that his noble grace would have some pity upon my wretched women, that so long have followed both my fortunes faithfully.

Of which there is not one, I dare avow, and now I should not lie; but will deserve for virtue and true beauty of the soul for honesty and decent carriage.

A right good husband, let him be a noble and sure, those men are happy that shall have them.

The last is, for my men, they are the poorest, but poverty could never draw them from me;

That they may have their wages duly paid them and something over to remember me by.

If heaven had pleased to have given me longer life and able means, we had not parted thus these are the whole contents; and good my lord, by that you love the dearest in this world, as you wish Christian peace to souls departed

Stand these poor people's friend, and urge the king to do me this last right.

Capucius: By heaven, I will, or let me lose the fashion of a man!

Queen Katharine: I thank you, honest lord.

Remember me in all humility unto his highness.

Say his long trouble now is passing out of this world, tell him in death, I blessed him, for so I will.

Mine eyes grow dim. Farewell, my lord. Griffith, farewell.

Nay, Patience, you must not leave me yet.

I must to bed, call in more women.

When I am dead, good wench, let me be used with honour.

Strew me over with maiden flowers, that all the world may know I was a chaste wife to my grave: embalm me; then lay me forth:

although unqueened, yet like a queen, and daughter to a king, inter me.

I can no more.

(Exeunt, leading Katharine)

Act V, Scene 1

A gallery in the palace. (London)

(Gardiner, Bishop of Winchester enters with a Page holding a torch before him, met by Lovell)

Gardiner: It's one o'clock, boy, is it not?

Page: It hath struck.

Gardiner: These should be hours for necessities, not for delights; times to repair our nature with comforting repose, and not for us to waste these times.

Good hour of night, Sir Thomas!

Whither so late?

Sir Thomas Lovell: Came you from the king, my lord

Gardiner: I did, Sir Thomas: and left him at primero with the Duke of Suffolk.

Sir Thomas Lovell: I must to him too, before he go to bed.

I'll take my leave.

Gardiner: Not yet, Sir Thomas Lovell, what's the matter?

It seems you are in haste, and if there be no great offence belongs to it, give your friend some touch of your late business.

Affairs, that walk, as they say spirits do, at midnight, have in them a wilder nature than the business that seeks dispatch by day.

Sir Thomas Lovell: My lord, I love you and durst commend a secret to your ear much weightier than this work.

The queen's in labour,

They say, in great extremity, and feared she'll with the labour end.

Gardiner: The fruit she goes with I pray for heartily, that it may find Good time, and live: but for the stock, Sir Thomas, I wish it grubbed up now.

Sir Thomas Lovell: Methinks I could cry the amen, and yet my conscience says she's a good creature, and, sweet lady, does deserve our better wishes.

Gardiner: But, sir, sir,

Hear me, Sir Thomas: you're a gentleman of mine own way, I know you wise, religious; and let me tell you, it will never be well.

It will not, Sir Thomas Lovell, take it of me, till Cranmer, Cromwell, her two hands and she sleep in their graves.

Sir Thomas Lovell: Now, sir, you speak of two the most remarked in the kingdom.

As for Cromwell, beside that of the jewel house is made master of the rolls, and the king's secretary further, sir, stands in the gap and trade of more preferments, with which the time will load him.

The archbishop is the king's hand and tongue; and who dare speak one syllable against him?

Gardiner: Yes, yes, Sir Thomas, there are that dare, and I myself have ventured to speak my mind of him; and indeed this day, Sir, I may tell it you I think I have incensed the lords of the council, that he is for so I know he is, they know he is a most arch heretic, a pestilence that does infect the land.

With which they moved, have broken with the king who hath so far given ear to our complaint; of his great grace and princely care foreseeing those fell mischiefs our reasons laid before him, hath commanded to-morrow morning to the council-board he be convented.

He's a rank weed, Sir Thomas, and we must root him out. From your affairs I hinder you too long: good night, Sir Thomas.

Sir Thomas Lovell: Many good nights, my lord: I rest your servant.

(Exeunt Gardiner and Page)

(King Henry VIII and Suffolk enter)

Henry VIII: Charles, I will play no more tonight, my mind's not on't; you are too hard for me.

Duke of Suffolk: Sir, I did never win of you before.

Henry VIII: But little, Charles, nor shall not, when my fancy's on my play.

Now, Lovell, from the queen what is the news?

Sir Thomas Lovell: I could not personally deliver to her what you commanded me, but by her woman I sent your message; who returned her thanks in the great'st humbleness, and desired your highness most heartily to pray for her.

Henry VIII: What say'st thou, ha?

To pray for her? what, is she crying out?

Sir Thomas Lovell: So said her woman; and that her sufferance made almost each pang a death.

Henry VIII: Alas, good lady!

Duke of Suffolk: God safely quit her of her burthen, and with gentle travail, to the gladding of your highness with an heir!

Henry VIII: It is midnight, Charles; I pray to thee, to bed; and in thy prayers remember the estate of my poor queen.

Leave me alone, for I must think of that which company would not be friendly to.

Duke of Suffolk: I wish your highness a quiet night; and my good mistress will remember in my prayers.

Henry VIII: Charles, good night.

(Suffolk exits)

(Denny enters)

Well, sir, what follows?

Sir Anthony Denny: Sir, I have brought my lord the archbishop, as you commanded me.

Henry VIII: Ha! Canterbury?

Sir Anthony Denny: Ay, my good lord.

Henry VIII: It is true: where is he, Denny?

Sir Anthony Denny: He attends your highness' pleasure.

(Denny exits)

Sir Thomas Lovell: (From Aside) This is about that which the bishop spoke.

I am happily come hither.

(Denny re-enters with Cranmer)

Henry VIII: Avoid the gallery.

(Lovell seems to stay)

Ha! I have said. Be gone. What!

(Exeunt Lovell and Denny)

Archbishop Cranmer: (From Aside)

I am fearful: wherefore frowns he thus?

It is his aspect of terror, all's not well.

Henry VIII: How now, my lord! You desire to know wherefore I sent for you.

Archbishop Cranmer: (Kneeling) It is my duty to attend your highness' pleasure.

Henry VIII: Pray you, arise, my good and gracious Lord of Canterbury.

Come, you and I must walk a turn together; I have news to tell you.

Come, come, give me your hand.

Ah, my good lord, I grieve at what I speak, and am right sorry to repeat what follows

I have, and most unwillingly, of late, heard many grievous, I do say, my lord, grievous complaints of you; which, being considered have moved us and our council.

That you shall this morning come before us where I know you cannot with such freedom purge yourself, but that till further trial in those charges; which will require your answer, you must take your patience to you, and be well contented to make your house our Tower.

You, a brother of us, it fits we thus proceed, or else no witness would come against you.

Archbishop Cranmer: (Kneeling)

I humbly thank your highness, and am right glad to catch this good occasion most throughly to be winnowed, where my chaff and corn shall fly asunder.

For I know there's none stands under more calumnious tongues than I myself, poor man.

Henry VIII: Stand up, good Canterbury.

Thy truth and thy integrity is rooted in us, thy friend.

Give me thy hand, stand up.

I pray to thee, let's walk.

Now, by my holy name, what manner of man are you?

My lord, I looked you would have given me your petition, that I should have taken some pains to bring together yourself and your accusers; and to have heard you, without endurance, further.

Archbishop Cranmer: Most dread liege, the good I stand on is my truth and honesty.

If they shall fail, I, with mine enemies, will triumph o'er my person; which I weigh not, being of those virtues vacant.

I fear nothing what can be said against me.

Henry VIII: Know you not how your state stands in the world, with the whole world?

Your enemies are many, and not small, their practises must bear the same proportion; and not ever the justice and the truth of the question carries the due of the verdict with it.

At what ease might corrupt minds procure knaves as corrupt to swear against you?

Such things have been done.

You are potently opposed, and with a malice of as great size.

Were you of better luck, I mean in perjured witness than your master whose minister you are, whiles here he lived upon this naughty earth?

Go to, go to, you take a precipice for no leap of danger and woo your own destruction.

Archbishop Cranmer: God and your majesty, protect mine innocence, or I fall into the trap is laid for me!

Henry VIII: Be of good cheer, they shall no more prevail than we give way to.

Keep comfort to you; and this morning see you do appear before them.

If they shall chance, in charging you with matters to commit you the best persuasions to the contrary; fail not to use and with what vehemency the occasion shall instruct you.

If entreaties will render you no remedy, this ring deliver them, and your appeal to us there make before them.

Look, the good man weeps!

He's honest, on mine honour. God's blest mother!

I swear he is true, hearted and a soul none better in my kingdom.

Get you gone, and do as I have bid you.

(Cranmer exists)

He has strangled his language in his tears.

(Old Lady enters with Lovell following)

Gentleman: (Within Area) Come back.

What mean you?

Old Lady: I'll not come back; the tidings that I bring will make my boldness manners.

Now, good angels, fly over thy royal head, and shade thy person under their blessed wings!

Henry VIII: Now, by thy looks

I guess thy message. Is the queen delivered?

Say, ay; and of a boy.

Old Lady: Ay-ay, my liege, and of a lovely boy.

The God of heaven both now and ever bless her!

It is a girl, promises boys hereafter.

Sir, your queen desires your visitation, and to be acquainted with this stranger it is as like you, as cherry is to cherry.

Henry VIII: Lovell!

Sir Thomas Lovell: Sir?

Henry VIII: Give her an hundred marks. I'll to the queen.

(Exits)

Old Lady: An hundred marks! By this light, I'll have more.

An ordinary groom is for such payment.

I will have more, or scold it out of him.

Said I for this, the girl was like to him?

I will have more, or else unsay it; and now while it is hot, I'll put it to the issue.

(Exeunt)

Act V, Scene 2

Before the council-chamber.

Pursuivants, Pages attending.

(Cranmer enters)

Archbishop Cranmer: I hope I am not too late; and yet the gentleman, that was sent to me from the council, prayed me to make great haste.

All fast? What means this? oh!

Who waits there? Sure, you know me?

(Keeper enters)

Keeper: Yes, my lord, but yet I cannot help you.

Archbishop Cranmer: Why?

(Doctor Butts enters)

Keeper: Your grace must wait till you be called for.

Archbishop Cranmer: So.

Doctor Butts: (From Aside)

This is a piece of malice.

I am glad I came this way so happily, the king shall understand it presently.

(Exits)

Archbishop Cranmer: (From Aside) It is Butts, the king's physician.

As he passed along, how earnestly he cast his eyes upon me!

Pray heaven he sound not my disgrace! For certain, this is of purpose laid by some that hate me.

God turn their hearts! I never sought their malice to quench mine honour.

They would shame to make me wait else at door, a fellow-counsellor, among boys, grooms, and lackeys; but their pleasures must be fulfilled, and I attend with patience.

(The King Henry VIII and Doctor Butts enter at a window above)

Doctor Butts: I'll show your grace the strangest sight.

Henry VIII: What's that, Butts?

Doctor Butts: I think your highness saw this many a day.

Henry VIII: Body of me, where is it?

Doctor Butts: There, my lord.

The high promotion of his grace of Canterbury who holds his state at door amongst pursuivants, pages, and footboys.

Henry VIII: Ha! it is he, indeed.

Is this the honour they do one another?

It is well there's one above them yet.

I had thought they had parted so much honesty among them, at least, good manners as not thus to suffer a man of his place; and so near our favour to dance attendance on their lordships' pleasures, and at the door too like a post with packets.

By holy Mary, Butts, there's knavery.

Let them alone, and draw the curtain close.

We shall hear more ah no.

(Exeunt)

Act V, Scene 3

The Council-Chamber.

(Chancellor enters, places himself at the upper end of the table on the left hand; a seat being left void above him, as for Cranmer's seat.

(Suffolk, Norfolk, Surrey, Chamberlain, Gardiner, seat themselves in order on each side. Cromwell at lower end, as secretary)

(Keeper is at the door)

Lord Chancellor: Speak to the business, master-secretary, why are we met in council?

Cromwell: Please your honours, the chief cause concerns his grace of Canterbury.

Gardiner: Has he had knowledge of it?

Cromwell: Yes.

Duke of Norfolk: Who waits there?

Keeper: Without, my noble lords?

Gardiner: Yes.

Keeper: My lord archbishop, and has done half an hour, to know your pleasures.

Lord Chancellor: Let him come in.

Keeper: Your grace may enter now.

(Cranmer enters and approaches the council-table)

Lord Chancellor: My good lord archbishop, I'm very sorry to sit here at this present, and behold that chair stand empty; but we all are men in our own natures frail, and capable of our flesh; few are angels.

Out of which frailty and want of wisdom you, that best should teach us, have misdemeaned yourself, and not a little, toward the king first; then his laws in filling the whole realm by your teaching and your chaplains, for so we are informed with new opinions, divers and dangerous which are heresies and not reformed may prove pernicious.

Gardiner: Which reformation must be sudden too, my noble lords; for those that tame wild horses pace them not in their hands to make them gentle, but stop their mouths with stubborn bits, and spur them till they obey the manage

If we suffer, out of our easiness and childish pity to one man's honour, this contagious sickness, farewell all physic: and what follows then?

Commotions, uproars, with a general taint of the whole state, as of late days our neighbours, the upper Germany, can dearly witness, yet freshly pitied in our memories.

Archbishop Cranmer: My good lords, hitherto, in all the progress both of my life and office, I have laboured and with no little study, that my teaching and the strong course of my authority might go one way, and safely, and the end was ever to do well.

Nor is there living, I speak it with a single heart, my lords a man that more detests, more stirs against both in his private conscience and his place; defacers of a public peace, than I do.

Pray heaven, the king may never find a heart with less allegiance in it! Men that make envy and crooked malice nourishment dare bite the best.

I do beseech your lordships, that in this case of justice, my accusers, be what they will, may stand forth face to face; and freely urge against me.

Duke of Suffolk: Nay, my lord,

That cannot be: you are a counsellor, and by that virtue no man dare accuse you.

Gardiner: My lord, because we have business of more moment, we will be short with you.

It is his highness' pleasure, and our consent, for better trial of you from hence you be committed to the Tower; where, being but a private man again, you shall know many dare accuse you boldly; more than, I fear, you are provided for.

Archbishop Cranmer: Ah, my good Lord of Winchester, I thank you, you are always my good friend.

If your will pass, I shall both find your lordship judge and juror, you are so merciful.

I see your end, it is my undoing, love and meekness, lord, become a churchman better than ambition.

Win straying souls with modesty again, cast none away.

That I shall clear myself, lay all the weight ye can upon my patience, I make as little doubt; as you do conscience in doing daily wrongs.

I could say more, but reverence to your calling makes me modest.

Gardiner: My lord, my lord, you are a sectary, that's the plain truth.

Your painted gloss discovers, to men that understand you, words and weakness.

Cromwell: My Lord of Winchester, you are a little, by your good favour too sharp, men so noble, however faulty yet should find respect for what they have been.

It is a cruelty to load a falling man.

Gardiner: Good master secretary, I cry your honour mercy, you may worst of all, at this table, say so.

Cromwell: Why, my lord?

Gardiner: Do not I know you for a favourer of this new sect? Ye are not sound.

Cromwell: Not sound?

Gardiner: Not sound, I say.

Cromwell: Would you were half so honest!

Men's prayers then would seek you, not their fears.

Gardiner: I shall remember this bold language.

Cromwell: Do. Remember your bold life too.

Lord Chancellor: This is too much, forbear for shame, my lords.

Gardiner: I have done.

Cromwell: And I.

Lord Chancellor: Then thus for you, my lord: it stands agreed, I take it, by all voices, that forthwith you be conveyed to the Tower a prisoner; there to remain till the king's further pleasure be known unto us.

Are you all agreed, lords?

All: We are.

Archbishop Cranmer: Is there no other way of mercy, but I must needs to the Tower, my lords?

Gardiner: What other

Would you expect? You are strangely troublesome.

Let some of the guard be ready there.

(Guard enters)

Archbishop Cranmer: For me? Must I go like a traitor thither?

Gardiner: Receive him, and see him safe in the Tower.

Archbishop Cranmer: Stay, good my lords, I have a little yet to say.

Look there, my lords, by virtue of that ring; I take my cause out of the gripes of cruel men, and give it to a most noble judge, the king my master.

Lord Chamberlain: This is the king's ring.

Earl of Surrey: It is no counterfeit.

Duke of Suffolk: It is the right ring, by heaven.

I told ye all, when ye first put this dangerous stone a-rolling, It would fall upon ourselves.

Duke of Norfolk: Do you think, my lords, the king will suffer but the little finger of this man to be vexed?

Lord Chancellor: It is now too certain; how much more is his life in value with him?

Would I were fairly out on it!

Cromwell: My mind gave me, in seeking tales and informations against this man, whose honesty the devil and his disciples only envy at; ye blew the fire that burns ye.

Now have at ye!

(King enters frowning on them; takes his seat)

Gardiner: Dread sovereign, how much are we bound to heaven in daily thanks, that gave us such a prince; not only good and wise, but most religious.

One that, in all obedience, makes the church the chief aim of his honour, and to strengthen that holy duty out of dear respect; his royal self in judgment comes to hear the cause betwixt her and this great offender.

Henry VIII: You were ever good at sudden commendations, Bishop of Winchester, but know I come not to hear such flattery now; and in my presence they are too thin and bare to hide offences.

To me you cannot reach, you play the spaniel, and think with wagging of your tongue to win me; but whatsoever thou takest me for, I'm sure thou hast a cruel nature and a bloody.

(To Cranmer)

Good man, sit down. Now let me see the proudest

He, that dares most, but wag his finger at thee.

By all that's holy, he had better starve than but once think this place becomes thee not.

Earl of Surrey: May it please your grace…

Henry VIII: No, sir, it does not please me.

I had thought I had had men of some understanding and wisdom of my council, but I find none.

Was it discretion, lords, to let this man, this good man, few of you deserve that title…

This honest man, wait like a lousy footboy at chamber door? And one as great as you are?

Why, what a shame was this! Did my commission bid ye so far forget yourselves?

I gave ye power as he was a counsellor to try him, not as a groom: there's some of ye, I see more out of malice than integrity would try him to the utmost, had ye mean which ye shall never have while I live.

Lord Chancellor: Thus far, my most dread sovereign, may it like your grace to let my tongue excuse all.

What was purposed concerning his imprisonment, was rather, if there be faith in men, meant for his trial and fair purgation to the world than malice, I'm sure in me.

Henry VIII: Well-well, my lords, respect him, take him and use him well; he's worthy of it.

I will say thus much for him, if a prince may be beholding to a subject, I am for his love and service, so to him, make me no more ado, but all embrace him.

Be friends, for shame, my lords! My Lord of Canterbury, I have a suit which you must not deny me; that is a fair young maid that yet wants baptism.

You must be godfather, and answer for her.

Archbishop Cranmer: The greatest monarch now alive may glory in such an honour: how may I deserve it that am a poor and humble subject to you?

Henry VIII: Come, come, my lord, you would spare your spoons.

You shall have two noble partners with you, the old Duchess of Norfolk, and Lady Marquess Dorset.

Will these please you?

Once more, my Lord of Winchester, I charge you, embrace and love this man.

Gardiner: With a true heart and brother-love I do it.

Archbishop Cranmer: And let heaven

Witness, how dear I hold this confirmation.

Henry VIII: Good man, those joyful tears show thy true heart.

The common voice, I see, is verified of thee, which says thus: Do my Lord of Canterbury A shrewd turn, and he is your friend for ever.

Come, lords, we trifle time away; I long to have this young one made a Christian.

As I have made ye one, lords, one remain, so I grow stronger, you more honour gain.

(Exeunt)

Act V, Scene 4

The palace yard.

(Noise and tumult within)

(Porter and his Man enters)

Porter: You'll leave your noise ah no, ye rascals.

Do you take the court for Paris-garden?

Ye rude slaves, leave your gaping.

(Within Area)

Good master porter, I belong to the larder.

Porter: Belong to the gallows, and be hanged, ye rogue!

Is this a place to roar in? Fetch me a dozen crab-tree staves, and strong ones: these are but switches to them.

I'll scratch your heads, you must be seeing christenings?

Do you look for ale and cakes here, you rude rascals?

Man: Pray, sir, be patient, it is as much impossible unless we sweep them from the door with cannons to scatter them, as it is to make them sleep on May-day morning; which will never be.

We may as well push against Powle's, as stir them.

Porter: How got they in, and be hanged?

Man: Alas, I know not; how gets the tide in?

As much as one sound cudgel of four foot, you see the poor remainder, could distribute,

I made no spare, sir.

Porter: You did nothing, sir.

Man: I am not Samson, nor Sir Guy, nor Colbrand, to mow them down before me; but if I spared any that had a head to hit, either young or old, he or she, cuckold or cuckold-maker, let me hope to see a chine again and that I would not for a cow, God save her!

(Within Area)

Do you hear, master porter?

Porter: I shall be with you presently, good master puppy.

Keep the door close, sirrah.

Man: What would you have me do?

Porter: What should you do, but knock them down by the dozens?

Is this Moorfields to muster in? Or have we some strange Indian with the great tool come to court, the women so besiege us?

Bless me, what a fry of fornication is at door! On my Christian conscience, this one christening will beget a thousand; here will be father, godfather, and all together.

Man: The spoons will be the bigger, sir.

There is a fellow somewhat near the door, he should be a brazier by his face, for, on my conscience, twenty of the dog-days now reign in's nose; all that stand about him are under the line, they need no other penance.

That fire-drake did I hit three times on the head, and three times was his nose discharged against me; he stands there, like a mortar-piece, to blow us.

There was a haberdasher's wife of small wit near him, that railed upon me till her pinked

porringer fell off her head, for kindling such a combustion in the state.

I missed the meteor once and hit that woman, who cried out Clubs!

When I might see from far some forty truncheoners draw to her succor, which were the hope of the strand where she was quartered.

They fell on while I made good my place, at length they came to the broom-staff to me.

I defied them still when suddenly a file of boys behind them, loose shot, delivered such a shower of pebbles, that I was fain to draw mine honour in; and let them win the work

The devil was amongst them, I think, surely.

Porter: These are the youths that thunder at a playhouse, and fight for bitten apples; that no audience but the tribulation of Tower-hill, or the limbs of Limehouse; as their dear brothers are able to endure.

I have some of them in Limbo Patrum, and there they are like to dance these three days; besides the running banquet of two beadles that is to come.

(Chamberlain enters)

Lord Chamberlain: Mercy on me, what a multitude are here!

They grow still too; from all parts they are coming, as if we kept a fair here!

Where are these porters, these lazy knaves?

Ye have made a fine hand, fellows.

There's a trim rabble let in, are all these, your faithful friends of the suburbs?

We shall have great store of room, no doubt, left for the ladies when they pass back from the christening.

Porter: And as it please your honour, we are but men; and what so many may do, not being torn a-pieces as we have done.

An army cannot rule them.

Lord Chamberlain: As I live, if the king blame me for it, I'll lay ye all by the heels, and suddenly at that; and on your heads clap round fines for neglect.

Ye are lazy knaves and here ye lie baiting of bombards when ye should do service.

Hark! the trumpets sound, they're come already from the christening.

Go, break among the press, and find a way out to let the troop pass fairly, or I'll find a Marshalsea shall hold ye play these two months.

Porter: Make way there for the princess.

Man: You great fellow, stand close up, or I'll make your head ache.

Porter: You in the camlet, get up on the rail; I'll peck you o'er the pales else.

(Exeunt)

Act V, Scene 5

The palace.

(Trumpets sound

(Two Aldermen, Lord Mayor, Garter, Cranmer, Norfolk with his marshal's staff, Suffolk, two Noblemen bearing great standing-bowls for the christening-gifts enter)

(Four Noblemen bearing a canopy under which the Duchess of Norfolk, godmother, bearing the child richly habited in a mantle, entourage started by a Lady follows the Marchioness Dorset, then the other godmother, and Ladies)

(The troop pass once about the stage, and Garter speaks)

Garter: Heaven, from thy endless goodness, send prosperous life, long, and ever happy, to the high and mighty princess of England, Elizabeth!

(Flourishing)

(King Henry VIII and Guard enter)

Archbishop Cranmer: (Kneeling) And to your royal grace, and the good queen,

My noble partners, and myself, thus pray.

All comfort, joy, in this most gracious lady, Heaven ever laid up to make parents happy, may hourly fall upon ye!

Henry VIII: Thank you, good lord archbishop, what is her name?

Archbishop Cranmer: Elizabeth.

Henry VIII: Stand up, lord.

(King Henry VIII kisses the child)

With this kiss take my blessing, God protect thee into whose hand I give thy life.

Archbishop Cranmer: Amen.

Henry VIII: My noble gossips, ye have been too prodigal.

I thank ye heartily; so shall this lady, when she has so much English.

Archbishop Cranmer: Let me speak, sir, for heaven now bids me and the words I utter.

Let none think flattery, for they'll find them truth.

This royal infant, heaven still move about her! Though in her cradle, yet now promises upon this land a thousand- thousand blessings, which time shall bring to ripeness.

She shall be, but few now living can behold that goodness, a pattern to all princes living with her, and all that shall succeed.

Saba was never more covetous of wisdom and fair virtue than this pure soul shall be.

All princely graces that mould up such a mighty piece as this is, with all the virtues that attend the good shall still be doubled on her.

Truth shall nurse her, holy and heavenly thoughts still counsel her, she shall be loved and feared.

Her own shall bless her, her foes shake like a field of beaten corn and hang their heads with sorrow.

Good grows with her.

In her days every man shall eat in safety under his own vine, what he plants and sing the merry songs of peace to all his neighbours.

God shall be truly known, and those about her, from her, shall read the perfect ways of honour; and by those claim their greatness, not by blood.

Nor shall this peace sleep with her, but as when the bird of wonder dies, the maiden phoenix with her ashes new create another heir as great in admiration as herself; so shall she leave her blessedness to one when heaven shall call her from this cloud of darkness, who from the sacred ashes of her honour shall star-like rise.

As great in fame as she was, and so stand fixed, peace, plenty, love, truth, terror, that were the servants to this chosen infant, shall then be his, and like a vine grow to him wherever the bright sun of heaven shall shine.

His honour and the greatness of his name shall be, and make new nations, he shall flourish and like a mountain cedar reach his branches to all the plains about him.

Our children's children shall see this, and bless heaven.

Henry VIII: Thou speakest wonders.

Archbishop Cranmer: She shall be, to the happiness of England, an aged princess; many days shall see her and yet no day without a deed to crown it.

Would I had known no more! But she must die, she must, the saints must have her; yet a virgin, a most unspotted lily shall she pass to the ground and all the world shall mourn her.

Henry VIII: Oh lord archbishop, thou hast made me now a man! Never before this happy child, did I get anything.

This oracle of comfort has so pleased me, that when I am in heaven I shall desire to see what this child does, and praise my Maker.

I thank ye all, to you my good lord mayor and your good brethren, I am much beholding.

I have received much honour by your presence and ye shall find me thankful.

Lead the way, lords.

Ye must all see the queen, and she must thank ye, she will be sick else.

This day, no man think he has business at his house, for all shall stay.

This little one shall make it holiday.

(Exeunt)

Finally

Chorus: It is ten to one this play can never please all that are here.

Some come to take their ease and sleep an act or two, but those we fear, we have frighted with our trumpets; so it is clear, they'll say it is naught.

Others, to hear the city abused extremely and cry: Hat's witty!

Which we have not done neither.

That, I fear, all the expected good we're like to hear, for this play at this time is only in the merciful construction of good women; for such a one we showed them.

If they smile and say it will do, I know within a while all the best men are ours; for it is ill happened if they hold when their ladies bid them clap.

The End

Description of Titles

The Comedy of Errors
Caught in a land of embittered woman and war, caught in months of strife, where a merchant's visit offers little natural relief. The fleeting moment of approving gold, inspire further bitterness, upon an approach to the marketplace, and then the women that occupy within them.

19 Characters

The Taming of the Shrew
Arrangements are made to spencer would be suiters to melt the splendors of a strong willed women. The winning is found pledged, influencing maids to seek their turns, and meanwhile terms required, an authentic spirit that they will/would wed soon.

34 Characters

Love's Labor's Lost
The house of a scholarly pursuit, returns into an expressive, either poetic or drunken as highlighting the gold-slur filled house of charms and dance like rhymes

19 Characters

A Midsummer Night's Dream
Journey into a land of fairies, where creatures are found to have the same issues as nobilities. Exemplifying, perhaps, there's no place like home. Meet fairies as they frolic and play the noble hearts and sway, posed in the recesses of night, and mystic lands of a faraway kingdom.

22 Characters

The Merchant of Venice

An angry Shylock brings to trial a merchant, over a lover's quarrel disrupted, demanding pounds of flesh. With no desires for even three times the amount, the Shylock demands his vengeance at heart.

22 Characters

The Merry Wives of Windsor
Mistresses and lords try and relate towards one another, as various important community figures come to have their word/seek the hostesses. Pleasantries are exchanged as a range of charms are expressed, until conversation resembled so to folly.

23 Characters

Much Ado About Nothing
Soldiery level consideration occupy the gossip, as several hostilities are summoned up, onto heart related matter. Also in conflict. The latter portion of the story lightens up to a women's home and pleasantries. Thereafter, a general search and care in actions, creating response phrasing poetic to the responses of leadership parading, until an end full of sensitivity asking gently questions, onto kisses

23 Characters

As You Like It
Troubled lower nobles venture about daily business, with some mild graces towards the ladies found. In need of relief or play, the Duke and family members take to the woods, where jests of drinking turn into troubled amusements, or warmth of a women's heart.

26 Characters

Troilus and Cressida
The infamous Greek battle for Troy. A large army arrives to take back the lost love of a humiliated foe. Both sides mobilize heroes onto the field, as soldiers and generals move to the side, and let strategies and fate take their course.

21+ Characters

All's Well That Ends Well
A tale of delightful, womanly gossip of a prestigious sort, until the French King has his word on the excellence of others. The story initially revolves around a strong willed countess, whose courteous pose and insight, reflect a nobility reflective of the house and court (council). Dialogue therein revolving around the councils rather, to exemplify (court counselling women).

25 Characters

Measure for Measure
Statesmen discourse leading with time to a personal reflection. Strolling Dukes and strong willed women occupy the background, where high-function status and family discourse intertwine within formalities (of administrative foresight, expression) observed.

24 Characters

Richard III

An in palace drama with King Richard the 3rd, Queen Elizabeth, and Queen Margret. Onto a haunting reunion, as the state processes royal executions.

61+ Characters

The Life and Death of King John

King John and Queen Elinor entertain the royal court, where a bastard has come to make his day. Strategic deployments of influence are exemplified, as the bastard plots about until alerts, alarm corruption has delivered trouble makers known.

24 Characters

Romeo and Juliet

Lovers emerge within a city gripped with two feuding houses apposed. As turmoil are caught in bitter heat, the lover's. Bliss and undying pledge becomes them, onto the eternal soul (of love and romance).

33 Characters

Othello

A hopeful Othello calls upon the favor of allies based on proposed merits, which called upon allies and foes to him. In a mixed response, allies and foes campaign both against Othello, becoming a bitter, personal tangle over a mislead love adventure representing the future of either fates

25 Characters

Macbeth

A desperate Macbeth ventures towards witches to tell fortune, returning to a castle haunted by ghost/old-spirits. Macbeth's worries become frightful nightmares, along the despair of the household around him.

39 Characters

Mark Antony and Cleopatra

The relations or affections of Mark Anthony and Cleopatra, onto the strategic interactions between Mark Anthony and Octavius. The discourse moves to the Octavius house, revealing Octavia, and later then, Pompey in the background. Overall the focus retains upon Mark Anthony, Cleopatra, and Octavius.

56+ Characters

Coriolanus

Citizens riot during a famine, while the state administrative intervenes and otherwise discourses the seriousness of the matter and war. Lady's calm the general ambience, until the sword is mobilized to defend the gates, , while the plight of people is nevertheless heard convincing Roman elites the problem is being found/fought within.

60 Characters

Pericles Prince of Tyre

A thoughtful/reflective Pericles interposes his good will and well-meaning nature, which leads him to visit fishermen friends, and onto state function. Pericles is then confronted, required to (take a plunge) to marry, embedding him deeper into ocean stock of sea life among sailors experience and merchant owners, investing his interest as babe, securing his destiny as then, future king

44 Characters

Cymbeline

Cymbeline, friend or loyalist to the first Caesars, is summoned into battle. Meanwhile there are personal matters to attend to within the noble house.

41 Characters

The Winter's Tale

A gossipy tale of high office, administrative daily insight onto the tender meaning of things and people an how they unite unwittingly at the discourse of their respected hierarchies of partnership. Profoundness therein inspiring the recounts of clown and child, as examples perhaps of what state administration and or nobility's company keeps.

34+ Characters

The Tempest

After an earth shattering storm, a fairy dwelling world is found. There magic and graces are there in song, glory and praises.

21 Characters

The Two Gentlemen of Verona
Loving beginnings, yet far too. General virtues going upwards in hierarchies, with overall chivalrous wits.

Twelfth Night
An evening in the company of sound gatherings, seemingly a docile manner recount version of noble delights. In similarities of the pose, composing an environment of insight and oversight.

Henry the 8th
Across chamber and palace, Dukes and lords, until Queen Katharine's and King Henry VIII's present their graces, conversing the Cardinal then. The signs then, an Elizabeth is born.

Richard II
King Richard the 2nd readies the armed forces at the sound of alarm, while later Henry IV is near for discussion. King Richard the 2nd and his groom.

Henry V

King Henry the 5th, as found across his palace, until a readiness for war. King Henry the 5th and the French King, with armies both have at it.

Henry VI, Part 1
Funeral of King Henry the 5th, Henry VI makes his approach to France. Henry VI fashions as thy lord protector.

Henry VI, Part 2
King Henry the 6th, where the Cardinal is seen mocking protectors with praise, as all the rage. Queen Margaret at King Henry VI, until the end.

Henry VI, Part 3
King Henry VI is busy fighting a succession of battles, France and England as having at it, yet again.

King Henry the 5th
King Henry 5 fight his way toward France, they reach the peaceful and loving responses of a French King.

Henry IV, Part 1
King Henry the 4th, from Palace to Pub, onto the battle fields again. Until there is no rebellion.

Henry IV, Part 2
Henry IV, from Palace, Priest and then tavern, he nevertheless finds some peace, after reflection. King Henry IV, and then King Henry V as fashionable by the end.

Titus Andronicus
A story of Romans and Goths, where roman sways give way. And then to see about Goths and proving worthiness.

28 Characters

Julius Caesar

Near the Final days of the 1st Caesar, and the continuation everlasting as through Octavius.

Hamlet
Hamlet, and his father the King, the father yet a Ghost. Hamlet, not so eager to join.

King Lear
King Lear, from palace to castle, to fighting the French in the field. After battle King Lear is in bed, the Doctor discourses, what lays then now, will have an impact upon the end.

Timon of Athens
A story set in Greece, a place of poets and cultured, good graces. From Arts and daily expressive, to political and charmed.

www.ingramcontent.com/pod-product-compliance
Lightning Source LLC
Chambersburg PA
CBHW071456080526
44587CB00014B/2122